DATE LOANED

W9-CNS-984

1cOct'33A

24 Oct'33F
6 Nov'33A

12 Dec'33A   14Mar'36N   2 Dec

19Dec'33T   10 J   '48

THE WORKS OF WALDO FRANK

STORY

THE UNWELCOME MAN (1917)
THE DARK MOTHER (1920)
RAHAB (1922)
CITY BLOCK (1922)
HOLIDAY (1923)
CHALK FACE (1924)
DAVID MARKAND   [*In preparation*

HISTORY

OUR AMERICA (1919)
VIRGIN SPAIN (1926)
THE RE-DISCOVERY OF AMERICA (1929)
AMERICA HISPANA (1931)

CRITICISM

THE ART OF THE VIEUX COLOMBIER (1918)
SALVOS (1924)
TIME EXPOSURES, BY "SEARCH-LIGHT" (1926)
PRIMER MENSAJE À LA AMERICA HISPANA
    (1930). (Published only in Spanish. Madrid and
    Buenos Aires.)
DAWN IN RUSSIA (1932)

THEATRE

NEW YEAR'S EVE (1929)

TRANSLATION

LUCIENNE, by Jules Romains (1925)
THE ANGEL OF SODOM, by A. Hernández-Catá
    [*In preparation*]

DAWN IN RUSSIA

DAWN IN RUSSIA

the record of a journey

by
Waldo Frank

❧

CHARLES SCRIBNER'S SONS

NEW YORK · LONDON

1932

COPYRIGHT, 1932, BY
WALDO FRANK

Printed in the United States of America

*All rights reserved. No part of this book
may be reproduced in any form without
the permission of Charles Scribner's Sons*

A

DK
914/7   267
F82d   F7
       1932

Contents

*Certain parts of this book in somewhat different form
were published in the following American magazines:
Harpers, The New Republic, and The Virginia Quar-
terly Review.*

190038

I
LENINGRAD

LENINGRAD

I

I needed a vacation, and decided—unreasonably perhaps—that I would have it in Russia. I salved my conscience by promising myself that my little trip was to be no quest for The Truth. I would see what I saw, feel what I felt, think what I thought: and since recreation means the turning from one experience to another, there seemed a good chance of my getting what I needed.

I did get what I needed; although it was not what I expected or precisely *knew* I needed. Yet the experience, however necessary, was perhaps too strenuous to be called a rest. Once again at home, I still felt that I must have that vacation. So I decided to take it by writing this book. Unlike my other books, I resolved not to work on this one: not to organize its materials, not to essentialize its form. I would let the book write itself.

These pages—of which as usual I write the beginning last—have indeed rested me; they have enabled me to relive—without the effort of the journey—a great adventure. I know that they may fully please no party. But perhaps, since they have satisfied a human need in me, they may satisfy a similar need in others who, like myself, are members of no party.

I boarded a Swedish boat for Gothenburg. I learned that Swedish food is the most delicious in the world. I learned that Swedish women have a grace, reticent and profound, which the male Swedes—practical roundheads—do not seem to me to deserve. I learned that Stockholm, under its low skies and bleak houses, has perpetual banked fires of human heartiness. In Stockholm, I saw Alexandra Mihailovna Kollontay, comrade of Lenin, Ambassadress of the Soviet Union. And while we chatted of Mexico where she has served, and of America and Russia, I found myself dangerously close to working on a problem which this woman vividly presented: the problem of the *person* in a collectivist world. Kollontay is, above all, warmly and deeply and clearly an individual. She is, of course, a product of old Russia—of the highly personalized culture of the intellectuals of old Russia. She is applying her genius, with so many other individuals of power, to the setting up of a world whose exclusive values are social. If Kol-

4

lontay and her comrades succeed, will the new Russia have *persons* as entire as she?

I reminded myself that I was having a vacation; and in order not to ponder a question so close to the main line of my work, I fled on to Finland. I had never thought of the Finns at all, supposing them an amorphous folk whose original Hun fire was probably long since quenched by Slav and Swede; a folk, I was sure, not worth stopping to see when one's Russian days were numbered. And now Helsingfors amazed me, put my ignorance to shame. Its modern architecture is superb; a few of its native paintings which I glimpsed have a Dionysian frenzy. And I marvelled at the women: their eyes full of blue distances, their bodies redolent of Spring, within these dour skies! But my visa into the U. S. S. R. was dated; I could not tarry and play with this new paradox of a folk oppressed by all God's inclement weathers—history and climate and a barren earth—who are yet so fertile and gracious.

I am the sole passenger in the sleeping car of the Leningrad Express. The conductress is a gray-haired, gray-faced Finn in whose eyes is the same fire I have felt beneath the glum façades of the Helsingfors streets. She has a smattering of German, and we converse. She tells me of the futility of governments and revolutions. But she smokes my cigarettes as if they mattered; and when I go to bed, she takes care that I have enough blankets.

2

Here, at dawn, I am at Rayayoki, the last town of Finland, the frontier of Europe. I get out on the platform. A funny old engine, like those which in my boyhood pulled the elevated trains in New York City, puffs into place. It bears the insignia of the Soviet Union; it pulls a Soviet mailcar (I laboriously spell the word), a Soviet baggage car, and a long "hard" coach empty but redolent of the massed humans who have filled it.

I smile up at the engineer, the first lord I have seen of the new Kingdom of labor. He smiles down at me, unconcerned; a bit complacent, perhaps. He seems strong up there in his throne of throttles and levers, I feel dispossessed beneath him. The platform is wide and empty, the station is silent and empty; I return to my empty sleeper feeling that I am in a spiritual no-man's land, here between Russia and the West. I have left a world behind me: what world am I about to enter?

The Swedish-German words of my Finn conductress sound far away, irrelevant. She and the European car—and possibly I—are a lag from a fading past. As the Soviet train attaches us, and lopes with us slowly into the dun plain of Russia, I sit alone as in a silence that I am bringing with me from the West into the East. I sit constrained, as if I am about to hear a Word for which all my life and all my past may have no answer.

The Russian frontier town is Byelo-Ostrov. While the train still moved toward it, a soldier jumped to the platform of my car.

"Tour-*ist?*" he said, pocketing my passport.

"No. Tovarishtch"—which means comrade—I replied.

He smiled. It was plain that he did not believe my nonsense; but from some height which he shared with the locomotive engineer, he also was indulgent.

The town did not look as if it had been carried along into the new world. It was visibly, not of the Soviets, but of Russia. The street was a broad swath of mud. Half a dozen teams stood mired in it while their horses dozed, hoofs in the ooze and head in the duga-bow, the flamboyant wooden yoke which, an acidulous Communist was to tell me, is the one thing the old Russians ever invented —and that thing useless. It was a thrill to see the classic duga-bow behind which the characters of Gogol and Tolstoy and Aksakov rode from Russia into the mind of the world. Along the farther platform were several hundred men and women, most of the latter harnessed to huge bundles. They were waiting, motionlessly waiting, for a train. They looked as if they had been waiting for hours, and as if hours did not exist; and as if, with the hard black bread in their hands, they might go on waiting peaceably for ever.

Our train was on time: Leningrad is only an hour and a half distant. But we stayed at Byelo-Ostrov for five hours. I took my little book of words, and whiled away the time with the soldiers and officials who, having carefully and vainly searched my books for contraband paper roubles,[1] were quite ready to smoke my American cigarettes.

There were about a dozen of us, soon, squatting on the station platform and conversing in a manner which I can explain only by the immediate group rapport between us. I know no Russian, and my vocabulary book, in accord with tradition, never yielded the word I sought. Among us was one girl: a young peasant with bare legs

[1]The paper rouble is artificially held at par by keeping it from all foreign money markets. Therefore its export, and of course import, is strictly forbidden; the visitor to the Soviet Union buys roubles of the government at the regular figure and can sell to the government on his departure those he has not spent. Nonetheless, there is a lively illicit market of paper roubles in Warsaw and Berlin, where they may be bought for an eighth or tenth of the legal rate.

9

and bleeding feet. She had walked long that day, with a load on her thin back. She did not speak, but she seemed to know what I was trying to say more quickly than the men. In a kind of song without words, we managed to commune on many topics. The American workers, did they have bread? were they going to delay much longer before they took command? The Russian muzhiks, how were they taking to the collective farms? Soon, I gathered, there would be no more muzhiks: and the Five Year Plan had already been telescoped into Four. What struck me about these men, and the girl too, was their good will. The good will of persons sure of themselves, sure of their place in a world that, being theirs, held no terrors for them. But although these officials of railway and of customs had the Marxist key to History and Culture, none could tell me why my car did not proceed to Leningrad. The train that had brought us was gone. The through sleeper stood alone in a siding, with the old Finn conductress imprisoned in it. "Soon" another train would be along to take us. I had my first lesson in the meaning of the Russian "soon"—a word as wide as the steppes.

The crowd thickened. At last came a train from some other point within the Union. My solitary sleeper was hitched to it. The other waiting passengers assaulted the other cars already packed with voyagers. They perched on the roofs, hung to the platforms, grasped the bags and bundles of those at least halfway inside. And the little loco-motive endlessly piping began to trot between sparse clusters of wooden houses. Generously wide, these first *izbas* I had seen appeared to me: paintless and dingy, yet always with carved win-dow-frames and roofs that managed to slope with grace toward the mud.

Now, the houses thickened. They became huge brick structures in bleak serration. The mud roads congealed into cobbled streets. Factories glowered red beneath smoke that hung heavy in the leaden sky. A dark-clad throng, more mobile than the smoke, poured up immense straight avenues whose angles our moving train kept twisting and flash-ing like the design of a *surréaliste* movie.

At last a wood platform spread beneath us, and ended in a wood palisade of gates and sheds. The cars burst open, pouring their human mass from door, window, roof, into the pulse of the prole-tarian city.

3

That first ride in a droschke was memorable. The cab's upholstery was mildewed, the wood was splintered; the izvostchik looked as if his prime had been the days of Gogol; and his horse, a poor relative of Rosinante, as if the Revolution had murdered all its friends and left it oatless. The Russian who met me at the station, after long bargaining, got the price of our ride to the hotel from twenty-five to twelve rubles—which means six dollars. This I found was a fair price, for the izvostchiks are bourgeois like ourselves, and have no ration cards. We crossed the Neva on the Alexandrovski Bridge and rattled down the Volodarskogo Prospekt.

As a rule, when I am in an open cab and newly arrived in a city, I note the buildings. Only later, walking the streets, do I come to a vivid sense of the people. In Leningrad, this experience was reversed. With effort, later, I saw the physical form of the town. Now, I was immersed in a tumultuous river of men; and the houses through which they flowed were like remotely distant banks. I had no time, keeping my head in the human current, to be aware of the houses. I saw them dimly, moldering gray, dark-windowed, although the long Russian summer afternoon had scarce begun to wane. I saw what had once been glittering shops: now dingy depots for some Trust, or empty. I saw the poorly paved streets. But all this with effort. For on the sidewalks were the people. Miserably clad, homely of face, their bodies matched the dilapidated houses. But the houses were frozen words of a dead past. The people were moving, their bodies, their faces, their hands, moving. And their motion through the Volodarskogo Prospekt was like an electric current, transfiguring them, giving them light. I felt this at once; but when the droschke tipped into the Nevsky Prospekt (now the Prospekt of October 25), the pulse of Leningrad was overwhelming. It lifted me from my seat (the more easily perhaps since I was perched half in the narrow cab and half in the air). I shouted to my friend to go on with my bags to the hotel, and I plunged alone into the great street.

The sun is gone. Soft twilight makes a single glow of the sky. Beneath it, beneath the jagged roof-tops, flows the folk. I have been weary: I have touched no food since breakfast at dawn in Finland. Now I am lifted up by a food I have never tasted. In these homely heads, these bodies miserably clothed, there drives a force that has the color of earth and the weight of earth, yet single and clear as the thinking mind. How shall I explain it? I have seen Negroes of the Congo dancing for hours: the hard rhythm of their feet, of their body muscles, of their jerking heads, is like the periodic beat of the orgasm—immense and endless. There is something of this dark issue on the Nevsky Prospekt. I have seen summer on wide fields, where cattle and grass weave together the dance of earth. There is something of this on the Nevsky. And I have sensed the thinking of a man, hard-eyed, clear-browed: he is faced with a crucial problem, suddenly he gets the line of its solution and follows it ruthlessly, beautifully, to its end. Of this also, in the pulse of the proletarian Russian street, there is something.

All the streets of lordly Petersburg are proletarian; and this is Revolution! The more conspicuous, since the old splendid shell of the imperial city has not changed. Everywhere the people and only the people! They sit in the Summer Garden, they stroll beneath the palaces of the Embankment, they fill the palaces figuring with obsolete abacus (the counting "machines" of China) at unpainted desks. Sumptuous streets are raucous with people, a family in each room; and the courts where ostlers harnessed equipages are now play-grounds for the children or woodsheds for the lo-cal tenants. What were once dainty shops in the Prospekts are government depots run by soviet clerks, crammed with workers. The huge depart-ment stores where the rich were reminded of the *Printemps* or the *Louvre* are co-operatives which only the elect—the people—may enter with cards. I feel that my first task is to see this people close —to look into the faces of the workers.

I sat down to rest in the Ploschad Zhertv Revo-lutzii, the former Parade Ground where the Tsar reviewed his troops, now dedicate to the victims of the Revolution. And there I sought my first "close-up" of the Russian face. About the tombs of the unnamed fallen, were flowers and frolick-ing children. Mothers nursed their babes, preg-nant women (with leave of absence from their factories) lazily waited their travail; workers on their day off (every day is "sunday" for every fifth toiler in the Union) watched the children with easy understanding and then turned back to their books—most of them on technical or Marx-ist subjects. I suppose there is no such thing any more in the civilized world as a naturally warlike people. But I can imagine the French, for instance, marching to war through pride or even vanity:

15

this folk of Leningrad, judged by my first glimpse of their faces, I cannot picture on their way to battle, unless first they were literally goaded. These typical town faces before me, what do they reveal about a people which has won its revolution? Men capable of bestial cruelty when angry; but not of the rational and abstract murder which is modern warfare. Men servilely ready to be led—even to their own destruction; yet who will never, of their own accord, form an aggressive army.

I learned later that this proletarian face of Leningrad is not typical of Russia. On the whole, this is a more conscious, more differentiated folk even than that of Moscow—vastly more so of course than that of the wide Russian worlds. Yet already here in Leningrad I begin to be puzzled by a contradiction. The face of the Great Russian (this is less the case in the Ukraine) is bland, childlike in its lack of sharp configurations: even the dwellers of the great industrial town seem to have the face of the muzhik. Its norm tends, as in the animal, toward the expressionless. Beside the face of the Frenchman—even of the French peasant—it is an unwritten page. But this face before me here in Leningrad has none of the dullness of the brute. Of the animal, it has the unconscious energy, the closeness to earth. Of the child, it has

16

the intimation of confineless promise. There is intelligence, emotional complexity, sensitivity of the spirit, making the face of the average North American or Frenchman by contrast a mere smart grimace. It has a quickening to abstract thought discernible in no child. And yet, when I attempt to localize these humane features in the bland Russian face, I can get no farther than the eyes. Perhaps from the eyes comes the aura of a potential maturity not yet writ in mouth, brow, cheek— even as it is not yet formed in Russian life. The Russian nose is often a snout; the face itself is as empty as the steppe; only when the eyes rule does the face grow wholly human.

I see already that all my brief hours I shall be studying the face of Russia: studying it, however, not with the will or the mind (I am on a vacation), but with the lazy eye of intuition. Let me dwell close to this face. Perhaps, some day, my eye will look into the eye of Russia. Then I shall begin to hear the heart of Russia. Perhaps I have begun already; for in industrial Leningrad, the will and forward edge of Russia, I see on the faces of the workers, despite their steep streets, the land's wideness; despite their rational order, the land's savagery.

4

Of course, not every man and woman in Leningrad is an industrial worker. There are swarms of clerks, hordes of petty bureaucrats. The banks, co-operatives, Trust and government offices, the courts and registries, breed their white-hand servants under commissars as under kings. But these for the most part are children of workers; their faces and bodies still have the stamp of the fathers who toiled in field or factory. And they are a humble lot, these petty office servants of the Proletariat. Even their portion of bread is smaller than that of the factory workers; and most of them earn less than a hundred roubles a month.

One morning, I stood outside the State Bank, at the opening hour, and watched the petty clerks and the important clerks swarm in. There were a few sons of the professional quill-sharpener whom Gogol painted in *The Cloak*—flea-bit souls, drab as their dress, whose gray faces and dim eyes had never seen nor been seen by the Revolution: creatures who were mere shabby pens for any will to push, and who had inconspicuously passed from the mailed fist of the Tsar to the steel hand of Labor. More numerous were decadent intellectuals —former lawyers, teachers, writers. Bewilderment was the one spark in their eyes. For a hundred years, their brains had been tenanted by confusions: now suddenly Confusion filled the streets of their city and they, unable to choose between the two dark sides of the barricades, were forced to choose by the one clear voice within them: hunger. There were scions of wealthy houses who had succeeded in hiding the shame of high birth that once was their sole possession. And there were women, middle-aged and middle-classed, once members of clubs, ornaments of salons. Within their eyes was hardness. They had borne their children, played their hour: now, obscurely, they were dead and their dead hands, remembering the skill of former years, traced figures which their eyes could never see, on Soviet paper.

The little army's clothes were a motley of the styles of thirty years. Some were dressed warm, some were in pale linens. But the faces of them all bespoke a chill, despite the mild weather, as if they lived in a perpetual frost. As they marched past me, in a hundred gaits—huddling, sliding, limping, pushing, shivering—one by one, with their caps and capes, their shawls and crooked boots, their relic slippers with French heels, their faded blouses and mended gaberdines, they gave a single rhythm: of submission. They were all slaves, now, of the Proletariat. They were all obeying. If the man above, who moved their hands, gave human orders, they would write what he dictated. If greed for power moved him, they would write what he dictated. Were they a disease of the old Russia, or of the transition? Would they multiply? And if so, might not their accumulated feebleness become the momentum of some new sinister bureaucracy? Could I be sure that the resilient life of the workers would gradually win them and make them over?

Wherever I went in the city one human type was altogether lacking—the conspicuous type in all the capitals of the world: *the successful,* the men who, by inheritance or luck or cunning, possess money, and who live for money; and the women of these men; and the servants (from footmen to lawyers, from priests to politicians) of these men and women. This dominant type, which had once filled the palaces of Petersburg and the great streets, even as they still swarm Fifth Avenue and the Prado, Champs-Elysées and Unter den Linden; this single dominant class that you will find in every restaurant and theatre and hotel from one frontier of Soviet Russia across the world to the other, was missing!

So profoundly strange is this lack in Leningrad that at first the mind does not record it. Workers —only workers: only humble men, simple women —happy or broken—everywhere! Not all heroes, of course: not, by a great deal, all beautiful or noble faces. Plenty of bestial faces, plenty of domineering, plenty of stupid faces. Every kind of face, as in all the world, except the face of money! Every kind of look, except that commonest look in the modern cities: the look that comes to the man and woman whose chief possession is money, whose chief devotion is the amassing of money.

I shall be ruthless in my scrutiny of the Russian people. But the rightness of my first joy in this has never left me. Faces that are sensual, faces stupefied by liquor, faces of a mere animal life— in them all there is a loam from which humanity may flower. But faces grown cold and sterile, living within high walls of money, are the faces of human death. What a joy to be in a great city where they have disappeared or hidden!

A day after my arrival in Leningrad, I found myself going about the streets softly singing to myself: I found myself humming while I shaved, I awoke with the song of my own voice. It was perhaps because of nothing positive which I had yet experienced in Russia: it was perhaps because for the first time in my life I was sharing the breath of a great city with a folk which has not fouled the air by perpetual forced incense to the cult of money.

5

The Hôtel d'Europe, where I lived, gave me a first feeling of what generous wealthy Petersburg must have been. The hotel is an enormous cave of memories. I walked through corridors so vast that murder or robbery could be committed in them with comparative safety.

My room occupied fully as much space as five single rooms in an American hotel. There was an ante-chamber, bare save for a giant cupboard without hangers, and a marble hatrack. There was a bathroom with a tub as long as a divan; but the water trickled so slowly—when it came at all—that I never had time for a bath. The bedroom itself was lofty and immense. In one corner was a porcelain stove that reached the ceiling; between the windows was a mahogany desk large enough for the president of an American insurance company. All other relics of greatness had been removed. In place of the canopy bed which the room called for, there was an iron cot with a single scrawny blanket, and a cracked cane chair. The windows opened on the Nevsky. The irresistible march of Leningrad beat into the Petersburg room, beat through the whole hotel. On these end-less halls thick carpets had lain; sleek pumps of a thousand lackeys had opened the great doors into the private suites; ladies in pearls, officers in gold lace, had caroused here, and plotted and loved. An advancing sea had swept all this away. The hotel was empty, the march of the folk went on.

But in the city the devastating work has been less thorough. Much of old Petersburg is here—dislocated but intact, to help me understand both Leningrad and the Soviet Union. I rejoice, for I realize that without knowledge of the matrix which is yesterday, I shall know nothing of to-morrow. Russia's Revolution, whatever else it is, is an organic life. The pulse of the people in the streets, fourteen years after the rising, leaves no doubt of that. The Russian Revolution must be a logical growth from Russian Tsardom. A success-ful revolution is always an evolution quickened by intelligence and will.

This capital of Peter was indeed an imperial city. The Neva is wide, its waters are steel blue. At the southeast it turns abruptly in a solid stream coming from Russia; to the west it forks and breaks among urban islands, seeking the Gulf of Finland, seeking the Ocean and Europe. The Neva gives many vistas, the spread of the city on its diverse banks is wide. In one distance are the chimneys of great mills; in another are the spires and darkling mass of the island of Peter and Paul with an Arsenal and a flimsy mosque behind them. On the south bank are palaces of the old regime —an unbroken elegance enjoying the river and fending the river's stately sweep from the hinterland—the proletarian city. Between these two hostile worlds, which never knew each other, lies an intermediate section—the world of the great bourgeois avenues with shops and banks and churches that spread a benison of gold upon the entire town; the world of the Prospekts with their theatres, their barracks, their offices and mansions. There must have been force in the old Tsardom, from Peter the Great to Alexander I, which in a hundred years expressed its power over the gigantic land in the very structure of its imperial city.

The lay-out of Petersburg was symbolic. The gray and rose granite of the embankment streets marks another world from the dark walls of the workers. Between these worlds a succession of huge squares holds the proletarian city back, and keeps it out of sight. There are no other squares like these in any city I have seen. The buildings, whose detail is usually baroque, are low; the squares give the ultimate effect, not of architectural units, but of *air*. They are *air-cushions*, fending the imperial quarters of eighteenth-century Petersburg from the nineteenth-century proletarian city.

When I stood in the Alexander Place—now the Workers' Garden—I felt, instantaneously, the logic of Tsardom—and its inevitable fate. Here is the Winter Palace, here the endless wings of the Admiralty building, here the convergence of three Prospekts. Since the houses are all uniform and low, their effect is a great silence like a regiment of soldiers at attention; their array, in open formations and wide avenues, holds the city aloof from the Palace—so immensely aloof, indeed, that it would have required a great imaginative effort for the Palace dwellers to *feel* the distant dwellers of the city.

No wonder when the people came here, in 1905, to beg bread of the "little father," he ordered them shot down. From his imperial demesne, cushioned off by the huge open squares, the toilers must have seemed to him small and alien and remote as an invasion of rats. Nonetheless, the rats defiled his enclosure with its architectural *cordon sanitaire:* even the Winter Palace, after 1905, was too close to the workers' city for that imperial ignorance upon which Tsardom rested. Nicholas II moved out to his own village, Tsarskoë Selo. It took another decade before this last retreat was invaded.

The method of Tsardom was, then, a deliberate aloofness made effective by the host of soldiers, bureaucrats and business men who, secured by gold and ease, kept the populace away. There is no relation of mind and feeling, no relation of spirit, between theocratic Petersburg and the city. There is no relation between the capital of the Tsars and Russia. Unlike the public places of other capital towns, the content of Admiralteysky, Dekabristov, Fontanka, Uritzkogo, Letny Sad, etc., is not the substantial stuff of the town itself, but a deliberate void. Yet there is a relationship of *energy* between the city and the vast system of squares and edifices fending it off from the imperial embankment. The immensity of every place, every dome, every palace: this is Russian. Tsardom's methods may have come from Germany, the styles from Italy, the absolutist ideals from Tatary or Byzance: but the teeming force wherewith the methods were applied could only be of Russia. Russian hands laid the lavish stones; the Russian soul—vague as the steppes—imagined the vast vistas.

This mark of the folk is even upon those buildings built on purpose to oppress the folk. Consider, for instance, the prison of Peter and Paul whose seventy-two solitary cells tortured, at one time or another, almost the entire company of Russia's revolutionary leaders. It is the most homelike of prisons. Its pentagonal stone shape is intimate and subtle; it is so shrewdly ensconsed behind granite bastions on the Neva and the Mint as to be almost invisible when one stands beside it. Its corridors have pleasing curves unlike the straight lines of Western penitentiaries. In the court are trees, in disorderly array, planted by prisoners on their daily walks. True, if there were thick carpets on the corridors, it was to keep the prison still as death, it was to enable the guards to steal silently to each door and observe the inmate. There was torture and heartbreak, of course, in the Petropavlovsky prison. But the collaboration of Russian energy gave it a personal complexion whose nature doubtless I shall better understand when I have been in the Union a little longer.

Now, the historic jail is a museum. Wax guards terrify you as you come upon them beyond a curve in the halls. Wax revolutionists languish on iron beds, tap furtively on the walls to one another as you peer in through the stout doors of the cells. The palaces also are museums (those that are not Soviet offices). The greatest churches are museums—either of ecclesiastic art or of ecclesiastic oppression. The Winter and Summer Gardens are toilers' gardens. The folk energy that made the buildings and the squares, imbuing them with its own abundance, has taken human shape. And proletarian Leningrad, which these careful structures warded off from the rulers, swarms the imperial city.

6

My hosts, as usual when Americans are with them, wanted to rush me at once to new factories, new workers' dwellings, new clubs, hospitals, schools. I was not quite ready. I put them off, till I possessed more firmly the dark background to which they of course, since they had sprung from it (*leaped,* rather), had to pay no heed. They were all concerned, naturally enough, with the blossoming of the flower; I longed to know the dark root.

I evaded my interpreter and my friends, and wandered into the maze of gloomy streets between Fontanka, Komisarovskaya Street and the Nevsky Prospekt. One day, I dragged my reluctant interpreter, who hated to waste his time on such unimportant places, to the Sennaya Ploschad—the Hay Market where Dostoievski's Raskolnikov had overheard the words which led to murder. The streets here are arcaded with rusty iron. Although it is summer, an organic chill broods under the gray houses (Petersburg is built on a swamp). Now, as in old days, there is a private market and the remnants of a ghetto. The folk come here to supplement with their spare roubles what their cards have bought at the government stores. Beneath the cellar-like walls are the *nepmen:* miserable creatures with hunted eyes, selling a carrot, a peck of apples, a rotten shoe, a torn umbrella, a lipstick, a bar of pale chocolate. I wandered through the maze, seeking its voice and rhythm. The vendors and the soiled walls belonged together; the buyers were from another world whose vitality I felt would burst these cerements of damp stone. I stood on a corner, automatically spelling out the name of the street to which I had strayed. *Stoliarny Peroulok . . .* the "S. Street" of Dostoievski, in which he lived while he wrote *Crime and Punishment,* and in which he lodged his hero!

This is old Petersburg. The wide gaunt gutter, the high gaunt houses—cold as an abyss, although the summer sun slants down the city. Misery has made the stones bitter, stiffened them into an organic hardness which no quarry can yield, which only man can bring into the world. And from the myriad windows on the street only darkness peers —the darkness of souls which despair shuts against light, since the day is light and the day is pain. And silence. Here, the Revolution with its tor-

rential pulse making a song of the street, is silent.
Here is the bleak root from which burst the red
flowers—1905 and 1917!

I find Dostoievski's house on the corner. My interpreter at last loses patience: he will not accompany me. So I go alone up a few broken steps, grope
through a blind hall and step into a court—the
dvor. The *dvor* of Petersburg is the heart of the
Revolution. And this one, from whose fifth-story
window Dostoievski—and Raskolnikov—looked
down, is typical and perfect. In one corner is a pile
of winter wood; in another sprawls an abandoned
cart. Half a dozen children are playing; but their
cries do not impair the *dvor's* silence: tier after
tier of window gloomily rising in gray wall, weav-
ing together the shut unity of silence. The court is
at once arcanal and vital. Life has long been
packed in this square body that rises a hundred
feet toward a pale sky. Only by bursting can its
life be released. The Russian *dvor,* like the grain
of corn, must rot. It is too hard for rotting? Then
it must explode. The subdued throb of the court,
within the stones, within the windows—I feel it
now: it is a throb of tumescence, promise of the
ecstasy of explosion. And I can see the great novelist looking down, partaking of the spirit of the
dvor. His Christian language is no longer in fash-
ion. But I understand the kinship between his

32

story of the *dvor* bursting into life by the release of crime, and the event that followed: all Petersburg hard and shut like a *dvor*, and its bleak stone flowering in violent revolution.

7

During the greater part of the nineteenth century, industrialism in Russia meant industrialism in Petersburg. The factory districts, of course, are on the periphery of the imperial town. Here, once, had been gentlemen's farms—great toy izbas, where the *barins* brought their ladies. As the hideous mills grew, the gentry moved out, and their houses became the first tenement slums of the workers. Many are still occupied. Around the windows are gay carvings; often the door is hand-tooled and lovely. But the black cellar is divided into rooms smaller than closets, and in each a family lodges. The rooms upstairs have likewise been partitioned, they are more like a storeroom than a home. All about on the unpaved earth is refuse and junk; the houses exhale the miasma of decay. But against these enemies and the vermin, the rooms are often clean.

New streets, grayer and harder and more bitter-cold than those of the Zentralniy, rise next to the old izbas. These date from the period after the freeing of the serfs, when Petersburg became an industrial city. And here are the new apartments built by the Revolution. They are drab structures of gray cement, hastily thrown up, often already crumbling after a few years' use. I saw more than one new house in which the plumbing had broken down and the walls begun to scale. Model workers' tenements in Gothenburg and Berlin are far more pleasant to behold, far better built. The Soviet hives are clean, airy—about as livable as a Bronx flat, although more crowded. Lack of ornament is as ostentatiously flaunted, as were the furbelows of Victorian days by our grandfathers. And the folk who live in them—one family to a room, with the father bunking on the floor and perhaps three children to a bed—grumble readily enough, despite the fresh air and the plumbing, of which none of them had even dreamed fifteen years ago.

The past is heavy upon Leningrad; not overnight can a folk destroy such dismal heritage. As I walked through the factory streets toward dusk I stumbled against drunkards in the gutter. There is still vodka. But although the visage of toiling Leningrad is forbidding, only an insensitive man could fail to note—even in the meanest quarter— the transfiguring difference from any other industrial city of the world. This folk have their heads high as they move through their streets. And when they invite you to inspect their tiny rooms, they have the pride of knowing not merely what they want—but that they will soon have it. The proletariat of Leningrad are a lordly people, still forced to live in the husk of the days of their enslavement.

In the Fontanka River, not far from where it rolls through steep streets into the Neva, barges piled with firewood are roped to the embankment. Like everything in Russia they are huge; yet the curved prow and the bellying stern make them— like everything in Russia—graceful. A small corps of men and women take the long logs, a couple of pairs of hands to each, and toss them to a couple above, who place them in rough order on the street.

It is the end of summer; the sun throws mellow heat from its far southern angle; but in two weeks it will snow, in a month Fontanka and Neva will have frozen hard and the *dvors* will crack with cold. The workers proceed in a slow heavy rhythm, ceaselessly. The men's chest muscles press against their blouses; the women, with faces more soberly aglow, have breasts so firm that the tossing of great logs does not make them tremor. They are women hard and sure, unmoving from their feet to their small heads, equalling their men. On the embankment, the crowd weaves. Every one is busy, no one is hurried. Save for the rare drunkards who stagger like wounded soldiers on the march, falling at last by the wayside while the march goes on, I see no idlers and no hysterically rushing men. The barge-workers are one with the moving street. The occasional motor lorries, slowly thundering by, are one with the workers. A detachment of passing soldiers sings a song of revolution that is like a banner flung to the sun, a banner that joins the sun to the human earth. Alone the houses bequeathed by the degraded past —the heavy heavy houses—are alien like winterfrozen banks of a springtime freshet.

One of the buildings just above a barge is a court house. As in all its kind the world over, the halls are packed. But this crowd is different. Here, no recognizable lawyers; no heavy-jowled judges sweeping with black robes into their chambers, followed by bald clerks with servile mouths; no sleek litigants of civil suits marshalling their witnesses, nursing their dollars, groomed by professional manipulators of human weakness. Here, the same human substance as the streets, as the barges, as the brigade of soldiers. Toiling men, toiling women. That little chap in a brown blouse before whom the crowd divides is also a proletarian. But the shape of his hairless head shows mind, the blue of his eyes reveals a penetrating witty flame. Perhaps he is a judge. I follow him into a court room.

On the benches that almost fill the dingy place are the people. Navvies, ironworkers, mechanics, a Chinese policeman, women. A group of intellectuals—probably clerks or representatives of some Trust—seem less at home than the others. The women vary widely in intelligence, not at all in clothing. There are servant types, drab and animal, there are daughters of peasants in whose eyes is a mental warmth as radiant as their bodies. The benches face a bare table on the same level, munitioned with paper and pencil, behind which are three empty chairs. On the wall behind the judicial seats, is a huge portrait of Lenin. Under it, in red letters, I read:

EVERYWHERE ALWAYS
LENIN
INSEPARABLY WITH US

(Lenin dominates the room, dominates the city. When I first arrived I faced his statue in the Finland Station: a huge iron "ikon" of the man whose squat body, long arms, enormous hands, seemed to catapult the cold steel of his mind into the massed workers. I saw the dainty villa of the

Grand Duke's mistress, the *ballarina* Kshesinskaya, from whose dove-blue balcony Lenin harangued the workers, gradually filling them with the intelligent hate that made "October." I saw the Smolny where Trotzky managed the "Ten Days that shook the world" and where Lenin came to live and rule in the first Bolshevik months. It is a huge bleak building with no faintest flavor of the young ladies who were taught in it. Only armed hatred, I felt, could storm it. Beside it is the Smolny Convent with its many-domed cathedral: the harmonious courts and dormitories are now filled with girls whose sole prayer is toil in factories, and whose promised bliss is to be proletarian brides. I felt the ruthless thrust of a mass power channelled in one man, that had transfigured the theocratic close into this teeming open garden. . . . But in the Smolny I saw the two rooms where Lenin lived. A humble place with a little iron bed and an old chiffonière and one upholstered chair and a kitchen table for his desk. Lenin still lives in these two rooms. And he is a different being from the indomitable force that swept the nation. This man is tender and caressing. A hurt dwells in him too deep for tears: but not too deep for a child's laughter. I shall understand the exterior of Lenin, his revolutionary city—iron, hatred, the cold plotting mind—only in these rooms where he lived. For here is his heart. . . .)

The side door of the court room opens, and my friend of the brown blouse quietly, without announcement, moves to the middle seat at the table. His two assistants, men of the mechanic class with honest kindly faces, sit at either side. At once, the place takes on an intimate air. It is a gathering of comrades, with work to do.

The judge turns his keen eyes on the benches and asks a question in a low voice. The Chinese gendarme and a blonde Slav woman came forward and stand at the table. She has been his wife, they are divorced, and there is a problem of some blankets: she claims they were hers, he claims that he brought them with him at their marriage and that he needs them. Blankets are costly and rare and terribly needed in wintry Leningrad. These people are actually fighting against a cold that may destroy them. The judge questions the Chinaman; then, without interruption, he lets him tell his story. He is a member of the Leningrad police, but his Russian is poor. No one smiles. For ten minutes he struggles patiently with the language; then stops. The judge and his associates have made a few notes. Now it is the woman's turn. She speaks more emotionally; her face flushes as she looks at her former husband. The judge does not interrupt her, despite her manifest detours.

40

His warm face is close to both the man and the woman, no hint of barrier or of social judgment is upon it. Each of the litigants brings up a witness, and these tell, in their own way, their story. In twenty minutes, the case is stated. The three judges retire; in five minutes they return. The judge awards the blankets to the woman. For the first time, the Chinaman's face reveals emotion: he is smiling.

The next case is called. A bearded man with clothes of a gentleman's past—plainly an intellectual—steps up. He represents the soviet of a factory of kitchen-ware in Leningrad. A shipment has been made to a co-operative in Vologda, which refuses to pay, claiming that the goods are defective. He tells his story hurriedly, concisely. When he has done, he submits a letter from the Vologda people. Rather than go to the expense of sending a man to Leningrad—a day's journey—the co-operative has put its case in writing and agrees to submit to the court's decision. The judge accepts the brief, and calls the next case. . . .

As I sat watching, receiving the essence of each cause from the unveiled human beings who embodied it and from the lambent blue eyes of the judge—scarce needing the help of my interpreter to understand—it came to me that this was the first court of human justice I had known. I have

witnessed hundreds of cases in my own country
(high courts and low, jury and equity), I have
seen trials in France, in Germany, in Madrid. I
have attended the open-air sessions of an Arab
kadi in market towns on the edge of the Sahara.
Of course, there were vast differences in form and
quality between these courts. I should say, off-
hand, that the American were the worst of all—
worst in the human value of the judge and lawyers, worst in the damaging barrier of legal tech-
nique between the human issue and the official
judgment: and that the courts in Madrid and the
Arab villages were the best, being the ones in
which the progress from statement to decision
was most humanly complete and least legally im-
peded. Yet in all these courts, from New York to
the Sahara, there were basic facts and premises
making real justice remote. The judge was of a
world apart from those who appeared before him.
In criminal cases, he was of a different class, having no honest contact with the defendant. But
even in civil suits where he perhaps shared the
economic and ideological status of the litigants
and their witnesses, his training both as lawyer
and politician, and his procedure as a jurist, kept
him essentially aloof from the human values
which determine the truth of the most technical
case. Literally, the judge knew nothing, and was

permitted to know nothing, of the intricate life before him. If he wanted to know, the barriers of etiquette, precedent, procedure, were so high that only an intellectual giant or an intuitive genius could surmount them. Here, these barriers were reduced to vanishing. Judge, pleaders, witnesses, were all one class. Statute was a brief, fresh page. Precedent was confined to the judge's knowledge of *human nature*. Communion between all parties was immediate and sympathetic. In my own country, the forms of judgeship are so isolating and so artificial that they must stultify any but the most superior human spirit: even a good mind will grow sterile in such a hedge of rules, and a weak soul will inevitably grow corrupt in such air of rationalization. But I felt that in this Soviet court, a fair mind would be challenged to grow strong, a weak spirit must be ennobled. For this judge could hide behind no tergiversations of procedure. He must work in the open—in the full ruthless human stream of uncorrupted living. If he failed to dispense justice, no system could protect him: his failure as a man would be plain to everyone before him.

Perhaps I had come, by chance, upon a Daniel. I suddenly took my interpreter by the hand, and refusing to be led, went down a flight of stairs, up a dark corridor, into another room. At the centre

of this judicial table sat a woman. She wore a dun
blouse in which her bosom was high. Her brown
long-bobbed hair framed the warm strength of
her features. She was young. On either side of
her sat two men in black blouses—rough fellows
older than she, with good eyes and honest mouths.
A girl of about twenty wept as she stood before
them and told her story. She had a month's-old
child and the man she claimed as its father insisted
there was another lover, who should share the
financial burden of the babe's support. The girl
denied the possible paternity of the second man.
The case held the room in absolute silence. On no
single face of man or woman was there a quaver
of rebuke, a flash of moral indignation or contempt for the girl. The case held the public, because it offered a hard practical problem. Would
one man or two have to help the little laundry-
worker?

The judge began to question. Mariusha was not
pretty, but her body within its damp gray shift
was like a morning of June. The judge called the
two men on either side of the girl. The first,
Ilyitch, whom Mariusha claimed as the father,
was a gangling fellow, tow-headed with thick lips
and a sharp nose—a baker. The second was a technical official in the laundry where Mariusha

worked. He was short and dark, clearly of bourgeois background—perhaps the son of some provincial bureaucrat of the old days, a man of about forty. His name was Gurkov.

The judge held the girl, at last, in her quiet scrutiny, as the three stood silent.

"You admit, citizen Fedskaya, relations with citizen Gurkov. And citizen Gurkov gets a good wage. If I decide he should share in the support of the child, what does it matter to you?"

"It matters! The father should pay. I will take nothing—nothing from any one else."

"But you were lovers?"

"Before Pyotr moved into the house. Then it was all past. It was nothing between him—the other—and me. Only last summer, in the laundry garden. . . . Pyotr is the father."

The judge smiled, as the human drama dawned clear in her mind. She withdrew with her associates; and in ten minutes they were once more at the table.

"Whether citizen Gurkov had sexual relations with citizen Fedskaya in the month of conception, we cannot positively know. Of the two who do know, the woman positively denies it and the man doubts it—although he is vague about dates. Even the alleged confession of citizen Fedskaya to com-

45

rade Ilyitch, claimed by the latter, is uncertain. In a fit of anger before she knew she was pregnant, she may have confessed in order to hurt the man I think she loves—perhaps in order to hold him and make him wed her. The presumption here is in favor of the paternity of comrade Ilyitch.

"But there is clearer and more directive evidence in another phase of the case—and we have been moved to our decision chiefly by this. It is clear that the true relationship here has been between the woman and comrade Ilyitch. Even if citizen Gurkov is the actual physical father, his relationship with the woman is of no importance. The attraction—and the contest—are between the woman and comrade Ilyitch. She wants *him,* not his money. She undoubtedly thinks, if he must support the child, that he will be forced to come and live in her room in order to save money. That is up to him—it depends on how saving he is." The crowd laughed, and no one rapped for order. "Besides, citizen Fedskaya's wish to fight the relationship out alone with comrade Ilyitch has a reasonable class basis, above the legitimate appeal of her emotion. Comrade Ilyitch is a holder of a card of the first category: a true member of the proletariat. We must expect more of him in every way—even though he earns less—than of citizen Gurkov. Let him meet the responsibility of his relationship, good or bad, with citizen Fedskaya. We adjudge him the father."

From the court room where a woman's warm voice called the next case to the embankment with winter wood piled high, from the packed limping tram whose overworked conductress every passenger was helping to collect her fares, through half the city—continuous bleak walls—we moved as in a single organism. Leningrad is a gigantic animal shaking its rugose hide as it rises from sleep. In the Volodorski district among warehouses, pipe factories, porcelain works and toilers' tenements, my interpreter and I sought a registry office of marriage and divorce.

In the waiting room were a number of young persons, a few more men than women. They sat on fancy carven chairs upholstered in yellow silk. The chairs were chipped and stained, the Chinese vases on the floor were cracked. The walls had been crudely whitewashed and were filled with posters garishly showing the embryonic stages of the normal child and the results of alcoholism and venereal disease in the newborn. My interpreter was a woman of about twenty-four, handsome, well-dressed (her husband was a physician and both of them drew good wages). As we went through the ante-room toward the inner office, the waiting group protested. What did we mean, trying to get married out of turn? Even if what hurried us was not marriage but divorce, couldn't we wait half an hour? My friend explained that I was not her future or past husband, but a mere "Amerikansky" writer, come to see the ways of the new world. How could I do this in an anteroom? The waiters were convinced, and we went in.

At a little desk in the little room sat a little girl. Before her were two huge ledgers, one for marriage and one for divorce. She was perhaps twenty-two, her hair was blonde, and a gold down warmed her naked arms. She smiled at us when she knew what we wanted, interrupting her questions to the man and woman that sat before her. She pointed to two Chinese chairs whose arms were golden dragons, returned to her ledger and in a moment dismissed the newly married couple. As they went out, another pair came in.

"Marriage or divorce?" said the registrar.

"Marriage," replied the boy.

She nodded them into the chairs, opened her ledger, and began her rote of questions: his name, his address, his race, his trade, his union, his wages, his past record of marriage, his freedom from venereal disease. She turned to the girl with the same list.

"Do you accept the citizen's assurance that he is healthy, or do you demand a doctor's license?"

"I accept his assurance."

"Do you wish to keep your own name or to take the name of your husband?"

"I wish to take his name."

The registrar put down the last answer and dismissed them.

They rose . . . a faint flush of joy on the girl's face, a faint regret within her eyes that the ceremony was so brief; and on the man's face a subtle discomfort as he felt the subdued emotion of his wife. Another pair came in. The squib of the little "minister" scratched and spluttered without end, dipped in the ink, recorded and recorded. She was warm with her exertion. Her shirt flared at her meaty throat. I was tempted to give her my fountain pen, pitying the ceaseless effort of that rosy wrist. And the couples came in, one by one.

In every young wife's face I saw that day, there was the same glow of tenderness and excitement; on every man's the same embarrassed protectiveness before his bride's emotion. And every bride, when asked the final question, answered: "I will take the name of my husband."

The marriage procession was rhythmically broken, every fourth or fifth interval, by a divorce. A man came in, breathless although he had been waiting his turn outside, usually unshaven, and announced his purpose. The little "minister" indifferently opened the second ledger. "Where was his marriage recorded?" "Had he been divorced before? or his wife?" "Were there children?" He sat, anger darkly deforming his face. It was so plain he was there as at the end of a tangent; his resolve was no slow deliberative growth but a sudden flaring need to be free . . . free chiefly of himself. Another man came in, silent, huddled, with red-rimmed eyes peering about. Only one woman sought a divorce: a tall girl with heavy hands and heavy head, with imperceptible breasts and a march like a grenadier's. A masculine type, rare in Russia, even as women who seek divorce are becoming rare.[1]

There was a wonder in the little room with its little clerk so sweetly human and so impersonally tying and untying knots . . . at seventy roubles a month. It was the essential human-ness, the full measure of feeling in each perfunctory act. We have learned that a good play needs no heavy "sets" to make it moving; give the actors the right lines, the true emotions to accompany them, and the bare stage will serve. That registry office was a bare stage indeed (except for the irrelevant Chinese bric-à-brac). Yet no couple coming to be

[1] In the years of War Communism, there was a wave of sexual license and divorce in the cities; it has now subsided.

wed failed in its brief scene to convey (as no church wedding with its trappings) the pathos and sweetness of man and woman who grope close to one another. And none of the single men coming alone to be divorced but brought with him the darkness that is so often the pitiful fruit of human groping.

I am neither defending nor decrying the Soviet system of marriage and divorce. I am recording what I immediately saw and felt. I confess, that before the impulsive anger of some of the men seeking divorce, I questioned whether it might not be well to guard them against an act they might themselves regret. Every married person has known moments when, with an office round the corner where divorce could be had for the asking, he would have rushed to it—and lived to repent. I wondered if a simple barrier of time might not profitably be placed against such angry moments: let the man register his wish, for instance, and receive his divorce only if he still wants it, after six meditative weeks. . . . But this is not what I wish here to note: merely the little faith of those who believe that alone the ceremonials of the past make marriage sweet, and men and women human.

There is intense emotion in Russia's personal life. Women here are women indeed. They march unafraid into the public turmoil; they work beside men in factory, mill and office. When they travel they sleep beside men, when they bathe—if need be—they bathe naked before them. They are unafraid of their bodies, they are so accepting of essential womanhood that they can forget about it when other phases of life absorb them. In their sexual relations, they meet men freely—spirit to spirit, unaided and untrammelled by conventions. Yet how womanly they are! how ripe in their tenderness and loyalty to their own natures! Here, in the Soviet Union, the Strindbergian warfare of the sexes seems to have no meaning. Here is no male will (the morbid will of the novels of D. H. Lawrence) pitted against a "terrible mother." Childlike and wise, these Russian men and women of the new age seem to share in the work of making it—in the ecstasy of peopling it. Each has what the other needs to share fully. "Let us work —and play—and let us love—together."

In all my stay in Russia, I saw one prostitute, although relics of the profession which once numbered scores of thousands in Petersburg and Moscow alone, still exist: their clientèle is chiefly foreigners. This wastrel of the old curse was on the Nevsky Prospekt. She made a sign to me, furtive and slight, and when I ignored it she made no other. She was utterly unreal in that throng:

she was like an exhalation of Russia's past swept instantly away in the fresh gale.

. . . But I am not ready for conclusions. As I move through my swift Russian circuit, I must delay conclusions. To judge is automatically to shut out or to limit impressions, in order to *form* the impressions already given. The time for this is not yet. Let the impressions, good and bad, come pouring in.

8

I am standing in the very cradle of the Revolution. It is here that the *Narodnaya Volya* (the People's Will), in the days before Marxism forced an organic method on proletarian despair, planted its bombs: here that Lenin dug the mouth of the subterranean passage which was to bring him, after twenty-five years of detours from Siberia to London, out into the light at Moscow's Kremlin. It was here that the first soviets sprang up, in 1905.

To all horizons from the Square lie the old bitter factory streets. But the Square itself has changed. All the buildings of former times are gone; the cobbled pavement has been replaced by asphalt. On one side is a huge Culture Club. The inspiration of these new architectures is Dutch; one cannot say that the Russians have improved on their models. The lines are ugly, the masses loom too heavy for the contours, the concrete is a dirty gray. Attached to the Club is a theatre; opposite is a great factory kitchen. The new structures have an impermanent air. They are like bivouacs of proletarian battle. Study them with standards of color and plastic and they are flimsy. Place them in their context—the jail-like factory streets, the Tsarist system ravaged by war and corruption—and they are admirable. Enter one of these Soviet mansions, see the men and women, the boys and girls of the Soviet morrow, and you will be convinced that the proudest building in the Union is not worthy of them; is indeed but a temporary shack.

It is supper time, the factory kitchen is full to bursting. I enter a huge hall holding a single male animal. Its parts are spread over benches and tables; it is guzzling coarse meats; its noise sways the chandeliers, bellies the walls and ceiling. Upstairs in smaller rooms are other collective creatures: one is comprised mostly of women and children—a few fond fathers; another contains mixed couples. All my training makes me wonder if the old worker's table in his private kitchen with his family alone around him was not more human. I know the arguments against it: the factory kitchen means better food, ampler food, above all, freedom for the women. Freedom for what? . . . Meantime, I have gone back downstairs to the main hall where the mass of men is feeding and roaring. My interpreter and I are invited to take seats and have a snack of beet salad and kvass. A worker who learned German in a prison camp during the War finds me and sits beside me.

The single thousand-headed monster decomposes—into human beings. I realize that each long table is a chain of individual groups: persons are everywhere, and speaking to one another. The din and the mass do not disturb them. They are at once impervious to that part of the crowd which does not concern them, and sensitized to what does. Talk as intimate and independent—talk as secret—as at any private kitchen table, flourishes about me. Yet the great communal animal is there, adding a dimension to all personal feeling, to all personal thoughts. Perhaps, too, upstairs, where the women who did not wish to cook, sit with their men and children, a new intimacy—subtle and strong enough to persist without private walls —is growing. Again, as with the new ways of marriage, I am forced to admit that only the form has ineluctably changed in Russia. Who shall dare say that the spirit which gives life to form—the eternal communion between man and man, between man and woman, between women and children—cannot survive in this still crude communal world? may not transfigure it and create for itself a fresh and healthy body?

I am struck, as I sit among them, by the sensitivity of the individual persons who make up this clamorous guzzling mob. They are all aware of me! As I get up to go, with the taste of the delicious kvass—brew of the black bread—on my lips, a hundred crowd around me. Questions! What is it like in America? What are the workers doing? When will they overthrow the Capitalist order? And war—is there danger of war?

These toilers with grimy clothes and heavy hands have eyes that rest tenderly upon me. Thus do children look upon those they trust: thus, animals upon men who have never hurt them. I am in the red heart of the Revolution. Outside, shells have ripped and scattered death. Yet these workers who with blood and iron have assumed dictatorship are gentle and boyish! When I picture the plight of the American worker who may have a shiny car in his garage and no pride in his heart, they glow with understanding. When I say to them, who have witnessed massacre and torture, "Yes: there might be war on the Soviet Union," their eyes grow dark with pain: they are like children warned that they may be interrupted in their lovely play of building a new world.

A cook and a waiter come up and explain to me that I am demoralizing the service with this crowd around me. This is an eating place; I had better go across the way to the Culture Club if I want to talk.

57

We work our way out into the Square. Decrepit red trams are disgorging; the grim streets are a flow of rhythmically moving bodies. A troupe from Stanislavsky's Moscow Studio is giving plays for a month at the Club theatre.

9

We have come to what was once a residential
street of the first class. The façades of the houses
still have pride and substance. But where the con-
cierge in uniform haughtily excluded all but the
best people, there is now a small state restaurant
at whose greasy tables proletarians eat salads of
beet and fish. Opposite is a government store with
its constant queue of women waiting for butter or
sugar. (We work seven hours for our bread, they
say in Russia, and stand in line seventeen hours to
get it). The thresholds of the apartments before
the queue have lost their elegance: masonry crum-
bles, carved doors are battered.

I explain to my interpreter that this is a call I
wish to make alone. Up four stone flights, an old
lady opens the door. Her watery eyes peer fright-
ened from her gray face. I give her a card from a
relative in Vienna, that vouches for me. Not
knowing what else she can do, she lets me in.

We stand in the wide hall of an eleven-room
apartment that once belonged to her and her husband, a prominent jurist of Tsarist days. Now ten
families fill it, sharing its bath and kitchen; and

the old owners are confined to what used to be their best salon. It is an ample room with a bed, a sofa, a miscellany of old furniture, mahogany and teak, and a clutter of pictures on the walls. My friends in Vienna wrote me: "Our dear Aunt and Uncle do not even want us to send them letters; they say their mail is opened and that even innocent letters from abroad get them into trouble with the GPU.[1] We are worried about them. See if they are in want. Help them. If they need money, give it." But Mrs. Z looks at me with the hard antagonism of a child who has been cruelly hurt. "So you have come to see the sights in Russia?" she says in excellent French. "Why have you come here? What do you want of us?" With effort I warm her mood, and her suspicions melt away in tears. With her tears comes the classic story of the Russian bourgeois.

Dr. Z, having at one time served in a non-political office, receives a pension of 100 roubles a month. Forty-three roubles go to the rent of their room. The balance is not quite enough for food, since they have no ration cards, belong to neither of the admitted categories of the proletarian world, and must buy in the open market at inflated prices. They survive by gradually selling off— doubtless to bureaucrats with an artistic flare—

[1]The Political (secret) Police.

their furniture and pictures. (All proletarians in Russia have plenty of roubles to-day. The shortage is not in paper money but in things to buy. Any common citizen will spend two roubles on a loaf of wheaten cake, or three on a stick of bad chocolate—and a fortune for a coat). So long as their reserve of bric-à-brac and furniture holds out, Dr. Z and his wife will not starve.

Presently he comes in, an upright man of more than seventy, with intellectual brow and a clear eye. His suit is shabby but his hands have grace. Even without the photograph on the wall, it is easy to picture them as they once were: the hautain officer of the Court and his tender bride. In them is the old Petersburg that stood between the palaces on the Neva and the bitter proletarian barracks. It was a Petersburg of brains and European culture: facing the palaces, serving the palaces, turning its back and its skill against the lowly streets. Now an old man and his broken wife stand barricaded behind the débris of their power —a few chairs and paintings—and give it piece by piece for the coarse black bread they once despised.

No glimmer of a sense of vicarious retribution troubles the jurist. He accepts the fortunes of war; he will die on his feet. He is an intelligent man, he knows it has always been war. Always he and his kind have given their wits to the palaces:

he accepts this scheme as he does the alternance of night and day. Never once in the thousand times he and his wife have gone to church has the thought come that because of his good mind and his culture, he may have sinned in not turning from the palaces, in not facing the other way.

As I sit with the rigid old man and his wife the ruins of whose face are still haunted by beauty, I am moved by these thoughts. If Dr. Z could but feel: *it is just!* If he could but say: "All the grace of our life and of the life of our class was distilled from the darkness of the masses. This had to be. It was the way, in all historic times, man has risen—by selection of the few, by physical exploitation of the many. Always the brainy men of the world—the men of laws and letters—have compounded this evil of the separation of man's spirit from the vast social body. Always they have been on the side of the possessors and against the dispossessed. But now, this is to be no longer! The masses are rising to take their place in the light which we, their masters, have laboriously created. We should rejoice. And if, rising in their brutality, the masses trample on us, this also has to be. I have been born in the hour when the historic debt must be paid. My part is to balance the account with the destruction of my personal life, with the sacrifice of my wife and family. It is hard. But surely it is not harder than the accumulated suffering of the people through all the ages. Let me accept my part, knowing its magnificent justice."

But no such revelation is in the face of the old man. The wonderful opportunity is missed. He sees merely the fortunes of war. He does not see that social revolution may be a sacrament, if the privileged graciously give back, with intellectual and cultural increase, what their fathers have taken.

At last I explain the main object of my visit. They refuse to be helped. Neither I nor their relatives in Vienna must try to give them anything. What should they do with dollars, except arouse suspicion? Let them be, the jurist courteously insists; and if need be, let them starve. Do I not know that every step I take is being watched; that this innocent visit may bring the heavy hand of the GPU upon them?

I left, fearing I had harmed the couple I came to help. In order to make them safe, I explained the entire affair to my interpreter whom I knew to be in touch, at least indirectly, with the GPU. I even brought her up and introduced her to the old couple. And I learned soon enough that their fears were justified. Non-Communist Russians were to tell me that they dared not have me in their rooms;

they were to show me their unwillingness (even when they knew my work) to speak their minds. The only frank criticism that I heard in Russia came from men who stood solid in the Communist Party. And I learned that the new secret police— the GPU—worked with an efficiency which compared with that of the old Cheka as a new motor car compares with an old droschke. Russia was at war, was in a state of siege. The two hostile worlds, since they could not understand each other, must fight to destroy each other. There were still those who secretly faced the palaces—who so naturally faced the palaces that they could never see the world behind them. And there were those who belonged to the workers. That was the essence of every human matter, from art and science to economics. All subtleties of emotion and of mind, all the nuances between truth and falsehood which make up the spectrum of human life, were merged into the single glare of Revolution, as the timbres of a vast orchestra may be merged into a military march.

I am beginning to see the human substance whose bare pulse I had felt in the streets. Even the first stage of the Communist Revolution—that stage without true communism in which the State with all its ancient habits of force and cunning still prevails and in which the proletariat seizes the

world with clumsy and unlearned hands in order
to remold it,—even this first stage is not quite
assured in Russia. The proletariat has beaten off
the Denekins and Kolchaks, it has cleansed the
palaces and commandeered the houses of men like
Dr. Z. But in positive values it is still feeble, as an
infant is feeble. Everywhere in the Soviet ranks
there remain lust of privilege, greed of power,
even love of money. That is why the dictatorship
is afraid of men like Dr. Z, who although starved,
are yet strong with the heritage of a millennial culture and with the inward unity that comes from
their acceptance of personal power as a normal
value. That, above all, is why the tone of the dictatorship is so shrill, why its intellectual propaganda is so violent against opposition, why its
repressive methods are so cruel. The Soviet Union
is fighting all that it calls *bourgeois,* not so much
in its enemies as in itself.

I thought of these words of Saint Augustine:
"When you think you hate your enemy, as often
as not, it is your brother that you hate."

He might have added ". . . and, underneath
all, yourself."

10

It was time to see the palaces.

Fifteen miles from Petersburg lay the Tsar's village, Tsarskoë Selo, carefully ensconced in a thick cushioning of noblemen's villas and gentlemen's farms. Now it is Dietskoë Selo—the children's village. But here still are the sumptuous homes built by Elisabeth, Catherine and Paul. Every Tsar, according to his taste, has made his contribution, preserving for the most part the work of his predecessors. And here finally Nicholas II made his last haven, after the uprising of 1905 had robbed him of the sense of security in Petersburg.

The palaces tell a plain tale of the decay of a great dynasty. When one recalls that from the beginning of Michael to the end of Nicholas there is a span of only 304 years, and that this brief day embraces the splendor of monarchs like Peter and Catherine the Great, the swiftness of Romanov decay and its ultimate degradation seem incredible. Only some organic flaw from the beginning (in the relationship between Russia and its rulers)—a flaw I must understand if I would understand the Soviet Union—can explain it.

The apartments of the Tsarinas Elizabeth and Catherine II reveal a magnificence less of empire than of genius. Versailles is paltry beside the imaginative splendor of this amber hall, this hall of mirrors, this silver dining-hall. Fantasy grown erudite is deepened here by natural intuition. The forms are of Europe's Renaissance, but the broad substance, the deep energy, is of Russia. In one room, there is a hardwood floor designed by Catherine's serfs. The wood is warm and melodious as an old violin; the theme is coldly and alienly classic. The vision, as one looks on it, is of pale Russian hands—exquisite in genius—hardened to sustain the heels of a Queen.

From this splendor to the home of Nicholas II and his Tsarina is an abysmal drop. The rooms are small and overcrowded with bric-à-brac and furniture that a prosperous iron monger of Pittsburgh would long since have relegated to the attic. The Tsar's study is like the "den" of a dull rich college boy of 1905—a boy never emancipated from his mother. Hunting trophies and military tokens load the tables. The desk and the walls are littered with family photos sentimentally inscribed in gawdy frames. The books are almost without exception heavily bound and illustrated works of travel or poetry albums or the type of novel found on parlor tables of Peoria and Cheyenne. The drawing room of the imperial couple is a chamber broken up into intimate cozy-corners. The pictures —including many portraits of the Tsar of all the Russias—are æsthetically on a level with the pastels sold in the basements of department stores. The walls are stained a sickly hue, supposed to be delicate and dainty. The ornaments, draperies and cushions are effeminate as well as vulgar.

The Master of Russia and his wife slept in narrow brass beds (you will find their equal in any Fourteenth Street furniture store), jammed close into the alcove of a narrow room. Over the imperial pillows on the wall are pinned more than six hundred tiny ikons. These had been gradually collected from the broad Russian lands for their unusual holiness and efficacy in protecting the imperial lives. On the opposite wall, at the beds' foot is the photograph of Rasputin inscribed to his two beloved imperial children: the long face of a fanatic, of a man shrewd, ignorant, passionate, cunning and sensually cruel. It, too, was supposed to be of help in guarding the sacred lives. But there is one other protection. At the Tsar's bedside, within easy reach, is a house telephone of the kind that was common in New York brownstone dwellings about thirty years ago. It connects with an ante-chamber where an armed sentry stood while the imperial couple slept. The windows are double. The garden beneath them is sunken; and here paced two soldiers to supplement the vigilance of the six hundred ikons.

What I have seen fills me with shame at myself. I thought I was going to glimpse the intimacy of a tyrant deposed in good battle by his raging subjects: and I have been prying into the privacy of an idiot! This pitiful little fellow with his hundred uniforms still tucked into a closet behind his sleeping chamber, with his prosy club-comforts and his sordid arts and his baby books and his tearful family keepsakes: this pitiful woman, his wife, with her vulgar tapestries and piddling what-nots, her passion for cozy corners and sacred relics: this third of the trio—Rasputin, degenerate priest and degenerate peasant—what sordidness, above all, what meanness! I can feel the redeeming trait of poor Nicky: he loves his wife and children, *they* are real to him although his Russia was more remote than the toy African jungles he loved to read about in his big-typed primers. I can be moved by the haunted mother-love of the Tsarina, a love that embraced her man in pity, that embraced all the household (this is why she chose to live in a small mansion), that perpetually fought the panic of her poor soul before the dark monster, alien Russia, they were condemned by an angry God to rule. I can feel the terrible beauty of the justice that placed these two in the hands of Rasputin, the insane sadist muzhik, making this man protector of the clique which ground his hundred million fellow muzhiks under heel. The world is salted by such irony, is cluttered with such detritus as these three sickly humans. But what of Russia itself? what kind of a world for more than twenty years can have suffered Nicky and his gang? suffered itself to be maimed, manacled, monarched, by such pigmies?

Where indeed is Russia? Have I yet encountered Russia?

As I walked through the revolutionary tide that floods from the factory streets into the Nevsky Prospekt, have I been in Russia? Must I perhaps leave Leningrad to enter Russia? I ride back to town from the old Tsar's Village—over the stone road laid smooth for the Tsar's horses and shattered by the tanks of Yudenitch. I am again within the bitter loom of the tenements. And I ponder this paradox of a mighty slave and his feeble master.

This much is sure. The Court of the last Romanovs was imbecile, because it was utterly cut off from Russia. Never was there the organic nexus that bound France and her kings, the Italian tyrants and their cities. The Court religion was also shrivelled to the maniac shape of a Rasputin, because it too was cut off from Russia, never were there the bonds of life and aspiration —unity of intellectual will—which for a thousand years made Rome the heart of all the Catholic peoples.

The great churches of Petersburg—St. Isaac, Alexander Nevsky Convent, Petropavlovski Sobr, Kazan Cathedral—one and all, Italian baroque or Byzantine or a bastardry of both—are utterly apart from the city; alien alike to its three sections: palace, middle class and slum. On the Griboyedev Canal between the Nevsky and the Neva, a bomb of the *Narodnaya Volya* killed Alexander II. And his heir, to prove his people's abhorrence for this deed, forced the millions of muzhiks to contribute their kopeks for a memorial. The memorial is the Church of the Resurrection. It is an imitation of the great Saint Basil's built by Ivan the Terrible, in Moscow. It is a ribald gyre of gold and sapphire and alabaster. The exterior walls are pieced in ikons, the seams are jewelled, the onion-shaped cupolas shriek discordantly against each other. This last church of the Tsars (it was built in 1881) is a caricature of Russia's spiritual body, even as the palace of Nicholas II is a caricature of Tsardom. And for the same reason, that it is a lie, that it is alien to Russia.

But the populace of Leningrad is strong and rhythmic. That strength cannot date from yesterday; it is too deep, too easeful. I think of the workers I have seen lolling in the villas of "The Islands" on the city's outskirts—enjoying their peace in the huge ugly mansions of the merchant millionaires, which they have taken over and filled with cots and books. I think of the crowds parading at night in the many parks, buying chocolate and kvass, listening to the sentimental music. I think of the great Pulse as I drove from the Finlandsky Voksal, which has never left me, and which so uplifts me that I am more ready here in Leningrad to sing than to stop to eat and sleep. This populace is strong and the strength must be Russia. Every worker in the industrial city is, after all, the grandchild of a muzhik. This strength—how could it tolerate the futile Nicky and his corrupt cohorts?

The answer is, that strength is weak until it is ordered; that Russia had vitality, not strength; and that as soon as its vitality grew ordered, became strength, it overthrew the Tsar. Russia, as an organic body, is new born. Peter the Great was dead less than two hundred years, when the rich school girls were driven from the Smolny. Peter conceived Russia. Before him, there had been Muscovy and Novgorod, and the amorphous tribes stretching farther east from Moscow than New York is westward. In this open immensity, there were no limits to give order: to give birth to strength. But Peter did not make Russia. He made an imperial system that took strength by sapping the vague vitality of Russia. Tsardom sent out its myriad slaves, to suck wealth from the muzhiks: the slaves returned like honey-bees with their loot, and the muzhiks remained sprawling in their continental mud. If they were Russia, and if their Russia had strength, then the ore still deep in the earth is finished steel. They had only the makings of strength.

In the early nineteenth century, order came into Russia for the first time: *the order of industry.* Factories gathered peasants into the towns: the old court of Peter became proletarian Petersburg. For the first time, the raw vitality of the land was formed into a body. And that body of Russia's first proletarian groups, the workers in Petersburg factories, was strong, and was at once a revolutionary force. But all the rest of Russia was still the prostrate chaos of the muzhik, from which the

Tsar's agents continued to suck power. In less than a hundred years, the few proletarian towns, with Petersburg to head them, achieved sufficient strength—which is human energy ordered and directed—to toss the Romanovs into the discard.

I begin to understand why this people worships the machine: why it is driven by so profound a need (a need whose instinctive force in every Russian no mere economic or political urgency can explain) to industrialize all Russia. Literally, the machine has given Russia birth. It was the machine-driven factory that crystalized the peasant, during the nineteenth century, into the revolutionary worker; giving him the form and ideology and strength of a social group. And it was the revolutionary worker—a few thousand in a chaos of 150,000,000—that moved the huge land toward dawn.

II
THE VOLGA

THE VOLGA

I

I am standing in a garden high above a city and a river. Behind me is a crumbled wall of many towers. This is the Kremlin, the citadel fortress. The town is Nizhni Novgorod, the river is the Volga. We have been here only a few hours, the minimum in Russia for getting anything done. We have breakfasted on the customary omelette and cheese with rye bread and butter and *chai*. We have found an official who promised to collect our reservations on the boat leaving this morning at eleven—which, he assures us positively, means three this afternoon; and to place our bags and coats and blankets in our cabin. "Let's go up to the height first," I said to Carol. "I want the lay of the land." We stepped out into Co-operative Street, and since the Kremlin hill is steep and Carol is tired, we decided to take a droschke. The street is a stratification—almost a stylization—of disorders. The housetops have a jagged line, the façades have an infinite variety of shapes and dirty colors, the pavement is not level, the cobbled gutter is a raised map of valleys and mountains. A battered American car of 1920 stands on the curb. One of the tires is punctured. The driver, without jacking up his wheel or removing the tire, is trying to inflate it with a tiny handpump. An hour later, having failed, of course, he will decide to bounce along on a flat rim. Here, in the heart of the principal street, is a church. It stands on a little height of unpaved earth; beside it rises a tower for baking bricks and all about are wood huts and goats and children. In this matrix of dust and anarchy, the church glows like a great ruby. It is indeed the famous Rozhdenstvenskaya Tserkov—jewel of Russian baroque. It is falling to pieces; the brick kiln wounds its façade and the shanties stifle it. And here is the cab stand.

We run our eyes swiftly over the choice of dilapidated droschkes, decrepit nags, flea-bit izvostchiks whose moldering greatcoats merge, a single substance, with their beards. They doze on their boxes, following us nonetheless with hungry eyes. We pick out a big blond fellow, who looks as if he could break his horse's bones in one hand and his flimsy droschke in the other.

"How much do you ask just to drive us up to the Kremlin?"

"Twenty roubles."

"Nichevo!" Ten dollars for ten minutes.

The izvostchik shrugs his shoulders and goes back to dozing.

I catch sight of a little man on the edge of the square. His red beard covers his entire face save for his eager eyes; and comes to a sudden point at his throat like the jest of a tragic story. "Let's try him," I say to Carol.

"Fifteen roubles."

"Why, it's absurd! Just to the top of the hill. We'll take the tram."

Just then, a trolley passes: it is gorged with people, men on the steps, women with bundles hanging to the men.

"What is fifteen roubles?" the driver wails, stretching out his hand. "Fifteen roubles nowadays is fifteen kopeks."

We know it is true. The poor izvostchik and we are of one class; both of us are *bourzhui* in proletarian Russia. Until the great new motor works just outside Nizhni begin to supply the cities with cheap taxis (they are beginning to come into Moscow), the government refrains from "liquidating" the poor horse-cab. It will go soon enough. Meantime, the izvostchik, Russia's last "capitalist"— for the kulak is gone—without ration cards, without co-operative rights, must pay outrageous prices for oats and stabling. He is a pariah. And as I look at the score of them before me, the cruelty of their slow death vises my heart. They are the salt of the old towns, these men smelling of manure, pungent with wit and irony, lovers of horses and vodka. And they are dying, they know not why. They know as little as their scrawny horses. They accept, like their nags.

We get our fellow capitalist down to ten roubles (five dollars, since I have not bought money on the *bootleg bourse*): and this is the minimum, without tip, at which I ever took a cab in Russia. We spread Carol's cape over the torn seat, squeeze ourselves in, and rattle up the hill. But at the Kremlin garden, our izvostchik refuses to be paid.

"I'll wait," with much waving of his hands.

"But we may be here for hours."

"I'll wait," he beams on us.

"We'll not pay you a kopek more, if you wait."

He looks half offended, half amused: what children are these, talking about "hours" as if they existed! He turns his body half around on the box. "I'll have a sleep." He throws down his reins (his nag is asleep already). He cups his head in his arm and silences us by dozing. We disappear around the garden edge.

The morning sun is high: there, spread in fertile haze before us, is a green plain whose nearer margin is the Volga. The cosmic scene has no true limits. The mist of the sky fuses in meadow, and meadow in river. On the river are boats and barges; they are long, graciously rhythmed, they too partake of the melodious vagueness. Only the town is different; its formlessness, below us, is sharp and hard. The world of plain and sky and water is a fertile quiet chaos; but the disorder of Nizhni Novgorod, whose streets are strewn about on bank and hill, is shut, hectic, splintered. I feel at once that the land is stronger than the work of man within it. The scene before my eyes is kin, not with Spain or France or Germany or Islam, where man in varying ways has drawn from his landside to create harmonious cities; but with my America where also, although differently, the towns are inferior and discordant to their surroundings.

The Volga is a sluggish flow, here where the Oka joins it. It is easeful, drifting down the world like our izvostchik; dozing interminably down into the Caspian Sea. I feel that it is poised between two worlds. The right bank, steep and accidented, where I stand and where the town adheres, is Europe. Beyond is the infinite flatness of another world. Asia! The beginning plain that does not end till the Pacific. The steppe, Siberia, Mongolia, the Gobi Desert, Manchuria . . . flat and limitless world: sea for nomads, tiding from the east against the Volga, against this barrier of Europe. And I feel an equipoise of forces. The Asiatic tide pressing from the east is balanced here by the high will of Europe, whose symbol is the Dyatlov mountain on which I stand. Horizontal meets perpendicular, and is equated. This is the Volga—and Russia.

If our boat leaves at three, we must hurry. Particularly since we do not know if the hour is reckoned by Moscow or Nizhni time—and can never *know,* although we ask a dozen persons. Sensitive man that he is, our izvostchik awakes at our approach. He peers at us from his dream with gentle eyes, as if his dream were so true as to contain us. We return to the restaurant on Co-operative Street, eat cabbage soup (the official has assured us we would dine on the boat) and turn toward the wharves.

This is the street, flanking the Volga, from which Gorki rose: these are the men and women of his dark stories. The Revolution is far away; but here are its causes. If there be a Russia, if Russia have a body, these are its bowels. In the centre of the street crawls an unbroken line of narrow carts—flimsy throwings-together of unpainted timber, with a man or woman squatting and driving. Each horse has its nose in the rear of the cart before it. In the shadow of the houses is a clotted maze of human beings. They stand or stir, they walk or totter; weary they sit on the curb, drunk they lie down in the gutter. They are a complex of motions frustrated into stagnancy. Their clothes are rags fantastic with stains and tears. Their feet are bound in straw or cloth, or bast: some of the women lurch in high felt boots. The men's faces are bearded, with hollow eyes; the women's features have been cut by agony. Want is the terrible constant of these people; yet —miraculously—it is external to them! It is a mold, maiming them, cutting them, crushing them, yet external. And from within, the fluttering of hands, the musical cadence of the wailing voices, the tremorous mouths of the women, the eyes of the old men, reveal a live observance of their world, half sorrowful thought, half jesting: reveal an indomitable spirit that belies the poverty, the ignorance, the degradation.

I feel, and am never to cease feeling, the paradox of Russia—its integral, pregnant contradiction. For these people are beasts; and yet a human pity, exquisite in grace, luminous in understanding, shines within them. These are men and women: yet their deeds do nothing to lift them above their cattle.

An old man has been watching us, now he comes up and speaks to me. He is drunk. He stands swaying, a potent fetid hulk in his wild tatters. His blond beard is streaked with innumerable potations, his teeth are black, his eyes are red. And his hands are hard and fouled like the hoofs of the horses dragging their carts through the mired street.

"Yes," he says, "look at us well, little brother. Stand very still and comfortable on this corner, and look at us well. Do you know where you are? You are in Russia. You are in the dark depth of the world—the darkest deep of the world."

Carol translates my answer, which he hears, not looking at her but at me.

"Yes, little father," I say, "it is dark. But I know darker places—places that are darker, because they do not know their darkness."

The man is a drunkard, a loafer. What dungheap must be his bed, what pig's fodder his hazardous meal? Yet as we stand in the roar of the traffic, he has singled out my mood and the precise form of thought of the American stranger. He has felt me, heard me, and responded to me with words darkly beautiful. It is true: the world of Tolstoi and Dostoievski is a true world. Who shall judge it?

We find Wharf Four, where our steamer, *Raskolnikov,* must be getting ready to take off on her long journey east, then south, to Astrakhan. Be-

fore a high wood grille are half a thousand muzhiks. Men lie on their backs, heads on hard
bundles: some sleep, some smoke, some merely
accept the throng and the sky in their unrespond-
ing gaze. Mothers, with boiling samovars before
them, have laid their children to sleep on rugs or
on the naked stone. Some have stretched out and
placed their babes on their breasts. In the arms of
some women lie their husbands, while other men
sit on bundles watching their sleeping wives, rolling cigarettes from scraps of newsprint, cutting
chunks of bread from loaves heavy and dark as
hardwood. Children weave in and out of the thick
throng, a crust of bread in one hand while the
other touches the grime and filth of their passage.

They are all passengers for the *Raskolnikov*.
Close by are horses hitched to empty carts; they
too are waiting for the steamer. Time and comfort
in the Western sense mean no more to the waiting
men and women, than to the horses. They have
been waiting all day; some have been there two
nights, having just missed the previous steamer.
They have no notion how long they will be waiting. It does not occur to them to ask. And even if
it did (an impossible assumption), they would
know what we do not: that they could receive no
answer.

At last we find a soldier who seems to recall

dimly that the *Raskolnikov* is coming to this pier. When will she come? He mounts obligingly on a wood stockade, and scans the upper river. He does not see her coming; how should he know, then, when she is coming? *Soon*. A minute, an hour, a day. We join this fragment of living Russia. Waiting Russia.

The Revolution with its orgasmic pulse is very far away. Are these peasants and proletarians waiting for a boat? or are they perhaps awaiting the Revolution? We wait. We have had, since dawn, only a breakfast and a plate of soup. But we are afraid to leave. There is a turn northward where the Oka joins the Volga. During the hour and a half we should need to return to the restaurant (in the next street) and consume a couple of eggs (boiled two minutes), our boat might come and leave. There is nothing to do but wait. And it is good to wait, deep immersed here, in Russia. Somewhere—in Russia—are our bags and tickets, for two cabins. Somewhere on the Volga is our boat. Somewhere in space-time is the conjunction of bags, tickets, boat and passengers. What is the hurry? I recall how in the novels of Dostoievski, people seem to drift from all over Russia, and meet in a street, in a house, in a particular room. I used to think these miraculous conventions were the licensed trick of the writer of detective fiction

(Dostoievski wrote glorified mystery stories). Now I begin to know that there lies something deeper in the necessity of these persons, spiritually bound, to come together in the flesh at a particular spot of Russia. I have abandoned my reliance on time. I am immersed in this plasm of the Russian folk. And as the day darkens and my head grows light with hunger, I begin to see as Russia sees: what destiny has joined life will cause to come together. Does this mean that human action is not needed? I will learn better. Human will, human intelligence, are part of destiny as the fruit is part of the tree. There is a time for action, even as there is a time for sufferance—a long time, and for waiting.

The wide twilight gradually shrinks and hardens; night comes down pale on Nizhni Novgorod. The embankment street still swirls upon itself: carts, laborers, loafers, eddying its stagnance. The houses stiffly retreat into the dark, their few lights blinking as if all Nizhni were a lamp whose oil is at an end. The Kremlin mountain four hundred feet above us has blazed in the refracted sun setting over Europe, and is now gone, quenched by the night that has come to us from Asia. We wait. The hundreds of huddled muzhiks grow more hushed. The last child has returned from its explorations to its mother. One crying babe is like the silence crying. The waiters—and we—are a single creature with legs and head drawn in to hoard its body-warmth against the chill of the world. The September night is cold. But we have a cheer of our own—the cozy reek of unbathed bodies, of old clothes, of straw and of human breath. A creature warmed by its own tangled fur, we lie between the city and the river, and await our boat.

It is midnight. All the women and children are asleep. Carol's head has fallen back on a huge peasant's bundle, she too is slumbering, with her cape drawn over her knees and her white throat bare. Many men are awake. Over the bodies of the sleepers, we wakers watch each other's eyes.

My eyes and theirs in the still Russian night on the edge of the Russian steppe—my eyes and theirs, together. I am far away from my own slope of the world, and these men speak a strange tongue from a strange past. Yet the world is a single clump of earth under our feet, and the skies are a single breath, and all tongues are variants of a single silence—when the eyes of one's brothers meet one's own in the night. I shall learn many *things* of Russia, and there will be myriad things I shall never learn. But after the night of waiting, I am close to this Russian human creature, close forever.

It is past midnight. The last samovar is out. Soon the sun will come as the night, out of Asia. It is very cold. The bearded faces glow faintly in the gloom; the faces are higher vibrances of the dark—they are the same substance more intensely keyed. From their sad eyes an aura drifts across the pavement. It is the spirit of human suffering abroad in the night. These men have suffered, all their race, tragically suffered. What I feel is not their poverty, not even their past serfdom. The pain that vibrates in their muzhik eyes is more terrible than these. I have no word for it; all I can fix is the sense of *a mortal deprivation.* These are men, and destiny has so far denied them some inalienable, some mortally needed experience of manhood. This explains why the mass about me is like a herd: animal, softly bestial. It also explains the hot and exquisite sensibility of these muzhik faces glowing in the dark—glowing in their dark: as if they were still struggling, with the essence of their humanity, with wit and will almost deliriously sharpened, to become free: not free as their ancestors were free before the days of serfdom, but at least wholly human.

I was awakened from a doze: there before me is our friend, the official. He presses two brass keys and a set of tickets in my hand.

"Now, soon, she is coming," he whispers in

English. And he explains how he has carried all our luggage to the pier on the left bank of the Oka—the "Siberian Harbor," where our boat (he calmly tells us) has been moored since yesterday morning.

"I have a droschke outside. Better hurry. You must board the steamer at the Oka pier. She is leaving right away. You must not board her, here."

I do not understand. We have been waiting on this street twelve hours, why not wait an hour more? But the man's excitement wins me. He sees something that I cannot see; I had better trust his Russian eyes. I rouse Carol, and we hasten over the sleeping bodies.

"Good bye, good journey," the official presses us into the narrow droschke. I try to place a five-rouble bill in his hand. "Oh, no," he says with eyes suddenly hurt, and then pitying, upon me. "Do you not know you cannot tip a Soviet official?"

The whip cracks, the hoofs strike sparks as the horse plunges forward: we begin to bound, toss, tip, over the crazy cobbles.

The houses are too sunken in a dream sordid and mystic, to give heed to us. We cross a bridge, we skirt the famous Fair grounds—a ruddy shadowed emptiness in the dim dawning; the wheels leap across unpaved dirt, striking stones,

crashing over holes. We dart between low rows of
sheds where the Siberian wood is stored and re-
distributed for Russia. We stop, so suddenly that
Carol's head and mine shoot forward into the
broad back of our izvostchik. Here indeed is the
Raskolnikov—and our cabins waiting. I forget in
my fatigue and hunger that hundreds of other human beings are still sitting or lying on that street,
and waiting.

This way of doing things may not appear human; but, as I am learning fast, it *is* Russia. Almost at once our steamer slides away from the low
sheds. Carol, who is an experienced traveller in
Russia, has gone to bed. She intends to sleep until
there is a chance to eat. But my hunger has made
sleep impossible. It is fourteen hours since I ate
cabbage soup; it is twenty-two hours since I ate an
omelette. And the hours have been filled with a
continuous intensity of labor; with all the intricate
integration of a hundred thousand percepts by
which I am coming to feel close to Russia. My
brain cells are bare and shredded, as if drained dry
of all their nurturing blood. And every nerve of
my body and face sings naked in the raw Volga
morning.

I grow aware of a murmur, then a tumult, then
a roar, as we approach the Nizhni wharf. The

night has gone. From the earth a luminous pall rises; the bodies of the city grow salient within it. I can see the peasants on the pier, with whom we waited.

Slumbering no more. The day of waiting is done, the moment of action has come. They are milling against each other like a thousand beasts. They are howling and pressing against the wood stockade that fends them from the river. Gracefully our boat slides in. The narrow gangway is rolled out, the stockade is withdrawn. And then there is enacted the scene, of which every landing on the Volga was to be a repetition. I understand why our good friend, the incorruptible Soviet official, although he was not loth to let us starve and freeze the whole night through on the river street, had wanted us safe on board before we took on the passengers at Nizhni. I saw the possibility that Carol or I might have been crushed to death; the merciful probability that we should have been pushed—merely—into the water.

The entire throng tried to board the narrow gangplank at once. It had waited twenty—thirty —forty hours: it could not wait another instant! Women with bundles were thrown down and trodden; boxes splashed overboard; children were separated from their mothers whose ululation rent the clamorous air. Men, gray-bearded, leaped on the shoulders of the mob before them and tried to climb the tangle of protestings heads; youths dug down into the knot of legs and skirts, pushed their way subterraneously forward. And rose a symphony of shouts, howls, oaths, objurgations, grunts and squeals, while the flimsy gangway groaned. At the ship's side stood two sailors trying to collect the tickets. They were silent, unconcerned; as if this incredible spectacle were customary—which it is.

When the last keening woman had found her child, and the last dripping bundle was salvaged from the flood, and the last ticketless youth (who had leaped aboard to the side of the gangplank over the gunwale) had been booted, good-naturedly, impersonally, communistically, back to shore; when the huge muzhik body was spread safe along the lower deck, sweating and steaming among the kitchens, the steerage and latrines, the sailors scratched a cool ear and drew in the plank. We started down the Volga.

2

I awoke at half past eight, having slept three hours.

"Good!" I said to myself, "it is late—I'll be able to get some breakfast."

I crowded into my clothes, convinced myself that Carol was not yet stirring in her cabin; and with my tin of tea stepped into the central hall. There was no one. I went aft into what was plainly the dining saloon. The tables were bare, the samovar on the sideboard was cold. I went out on deck. The right bank was rolling hills, wooded and smiling. Europe. The left bank spread sere from its sands into the low horizon of Asia. I went down the companionway. The entire lower boat was stifled with peasants. Outside, they slept among packing boxes, they lay amid cordage, machinery and anchors. In the hold, they lay in tiers of wooden shelves, and on the floor shiny with oil. Most of them were asleep, and as my senses grew accustomed to the fetor, my eyes to the darkness, I could see their faces. Contented sleeping faces.

Even the old folks lying on wet wood with a crow-bar for a pillow were comfortably resting. A few who were awake were munching apples. Rotten little apples, the kind we would feed to pigs.

I watched one woman. She had a score of apples in her lap. She picked up one and without looking at it sank her teeth into the black decay. There was not a sound spot on that apple. Yet the woman's teeth were white and her flesh was firm and her eyes shone blue. I found myself envying the woman who was so free and strong that she could enjoy rotted apples. I found myself questioning the wisdom of my own fastidiousness. Before I knew what I was doing, I thrust a rouble into the woman's hand and pointed to the apples. She arose and in a moment returned with a basketful of the fruit. Laughing, she began to stuff apples into my coat, into my cap, and the last ones she emptied into my arms. Finally she took a handful of coppers, counted my change laboriously, and slipped the coins into my bulging pocket. I stumbled upstairs to examine my purchase. I had thirty apples, all of them small and most of them rotten. I was hungry, and I envied the muzhiks more than ever. But I could not eat the apples.

We were approaching a village. At the embankment a mud road filled with carts and a solid mass of peasants. On either side of the road, small booths of unpainted wood in which I could see the bearded face of a man or the shawled bland face of a woman. The road swung to the right and mounted the hill. The izbas were large with slanting roof, and always the window frames featly carved. At the top of the hill they spread into a streetless scatter. They were of wood, and gracefully at one with their earth and their sky. But above them rose a brick church with an onion-shaped dome of gilded zinc. It was a gaunt and hideous intruder, having no kinship with the wooden village or with the wooded earth.

The boat docked to the same scene I was to witness—or to hear in my sleep—each time we made a landing. Before the gangway were massed a hundred muzhiks ready to get off, and a pile of freight that had to be disembarked. On the pier, equally massed, were a hundred other muzhiks, and crates of vegetables, bags of potatoes, destined for Samara or Stalingrad. At once pandemonium. Muzhiks leaving met crates coming on; boxes unloading clashed with muzhiks trying to board. The simple business became a battle. The porters, already heavily burdened, had to fight their way against passengers, and passengers had to use their bodies and their hands against each other and against obstructing vegetables and potatoes. Women were trampled, produce was scattered and ruined. Yet the roaring spectacle was without hard feeling. Men wrestled, pummelled, pushed— with no personal animus against the body or the crate that was their sudden foe. And eventually the newcomers were all on board, and the new arrivals were all landed. The tumult, which had rung like a war to the death, died into a peace that had no memory of trouble. The boat slid again into the Volga.

I reconnoitred the kitchen once more, and the dining room. It was nine thirty. Carol, who knows how to voyage in Russia, was still blithely asleep. My stomach had become a flame, white and ravaging within me. I found a mechanic on his way to Stalingrad, a dark lustful proletarian from the Ukraine who knew some German. He looked at me reproachfully when I told him I was hungry. Of course, there would be breakfast. When? Oh, around noon, perhaps: what did it matter? I found the girl in whose little buxom person was centred the multiple business of waiting on the table, making out bills and collecting money—and cleaning all the cabins. Ilyena was perhaps sixteen, full-cheeked, full-breasted, with motherly blue eyes. I came to admire Ilyena. Her work was ceaseless, and so was her good humor. Not three European women—not five American women, could have done what she did. I told her that I was literally starving: and Ilyena brought me a samovar of hot water.

I sat down in the empty saloon, and learned the miracle of tea. Never will I forget that glass in which, slowly, I poured the fluid, adding my own leaves, and a spoonful of coarse sugar. It did not taste good, it did not taste at all: it was a transfiguring force! Once more I was a man with a clear head, with a body that moved as my head ordered. The tea did not dispel my hunger; it made me again a reasonable although hungry person.

I took a knife, peeled and pruned a dozen of my less rotten apples, and ate them. Now my hunger was a ravaging flame no more: it was a mere sharp blade, cutting my body. All it needed was to be dulled.

At the next landing, I let myself be swept ashore with the scrimmage. I stood on the fertile mud of Russia. I bought a loaf of black bread at a booth, and wandered up into the village. The bread was heavy, damp, sour. It was delicious. It tasted like the village. From the soil, a haze rose to the sky, a burden of fertility half loam, half sun. Within the warm mist-substance, and of it, were the village beasts, were the children, were the houses and men and women. Here was a homogeneous world: man and animal and fruit, air and wood and earth, were a simple substance whose parts slowly vibrated round its core—the sun. The Russian village! For ages it had stood like a great tree with its roots in Russia, and had grown like a tree, and had stirred only as a tree stirs. But now it was doomed. Revolution was uprooting it. I knew why there was this frantic movement of the muzhiks up and down the Volga. The *kolhoz* (collective farm) and the *sovhoz* (state farm) were fighting the old village to the death. By millions, the muzhiks were being forced into vast proletarianized "works" for the "manufacture" of wheat or potatoes. Last year, they had been forced by violence. Civil war had raged up and down the Volga, until Stalin changed his tactics from gunfire to the subtler methods of moral and economic pressure.

How the muzhik felt, I could feel as I stood in the village mud and sensed the organic rhythm of this telluric world—the pulse of earth and beast and man together. And I understood the message of the scene at each landing. The muzhik was indeed like an animal: he lived rhythmically so long as he lived within the form of his instinctive life. Getting on and off a steamer was not part of his traditional equipment. He was lost in this strange process, as his cow would have been lost without a driver. I began to see the immensity of the task which revolutionary Russia had undertaken. The

99

190038

organic pulse of the Leningrad workers a thousand miles to the west—would it be strong enough to transfigure these muzhiks? Only if it did, could revolutionary Russia become an organic body. Only if it did, could the Revolution survive.

3

As we sailed east almost into the shadow of the Urals, the Revolution shrank smaller, farther, unreal away. Even in my sleep in Leningrad its beat, bursting the old world, was in my ears and I had waked each morning to its thunderous music. Now, while we stopped at village after village, there were whole hours when I forgot the Revolution, when I knew only Russia. For if the migrating muzhik was a sign of Russia's deepest move— the proletarianizing of the farm, as yet the hearts of these men and women, despite the destiny of their bodies, knew no Revolution.

We stopped at villages in the Mari region and the Chuvash Republic: a Finnish folk, kin to Hun and Turk, stormed the lower deck. We came to the autonomous republic of the Tatars. Here the slant eyes of the Mongol plain beyond Siberia stared at me, as I wandered up the village street. The left bank had been growing steadily more arid and more flat. Now, it was steppe: the true half-desert sweep of Asia was upon us, was even leaping the Volga into Europe. On the right bank, the villages in their hilly contours had recalled hamlets of Hungary and Bohemia: true outposts of Central Europe despite the differing details of their broad crude izbas, and of their alien churches (the church of a Catholic village is harmonious with its houses). Now, the villages stood bleak and dry. The mellow wooden izba turned into gaunt stone. Camels were hitched to Russian carts. Women still wore felt boots like their Slav sisters; but they swathed black shawls about their bodies like their sisters of Islam, and their eyes slanted toward China.

Russia's Völkerchaos! At Kazan, the Tatar capital, I plunged within it. Chaos is Russia's body —a body that centuries have not aged, even as untilled soil does not age. And order out of chaos is Russia's will—a will young as the Revolution, heroic and tragic as revolution. I met them both— body and will—at Kazan.

On the horizon is a tower that was once the mosque of the Khan Sunbeka; and is the Kremlin wall built by Ivan the Terrible when he captured Kazan and made it Christian. Long before the Tatars, the Bulgars were here; first they were pagan, then Islam won them. And although they have left no minarets like the Tatars, I felt them also—their southern sultriness meeting the Mongol calm and the Muscovite passion, in that thick fever of moods which is the air of Kazan.

Up and down the Volga for a thousand years, the races have swirled in battle as tortuous as the course of the great river. Turanian, Slav, Semite, Iranian, Mongol, Slav again. . . . They came down from the Baltic into Muscovy and into the Caspian: they came up from Persia, Afghanistan and Iraq, into Muscovy, into the Baltic; they came from the Tatar east, they came from the west Danube. And always they came by the Volga: on the Volga they fought, advanced, retreated: on the Volga they lived. The Volgaland, which has seen a thousand invasions—where only yesterday the White Czecho-slovaks held Kazan and where Kolchak raged—is the symbol of Russia's chaos. It has no boundaries, it is open to all four winds. Therefore it has remained a chaos. Its muzhiks rooted only as trees take root: in their *humanity* they are unorganized and chaotic. Its townfolk— Nizhni Novgorod, Simbirsk, Samara, Saratov, Tsaritzin—settled only in terms of their dingy daily life: culturally, they remained unformed, remained in a stratified chaos of which their cities, disordered and set, are the symbol.

Every group of men, however vital, to become creative must be *cross-fertilized* by some outside group. There is no parthenogenesis in the biology of human culture. But none of the outside cultural forces which in the past swept the Russian plain was strong enough to bring this organic human order to the Slav's slumberous chaos. Not Islam, whose fecundity waned as it spread north. Not Byzance, although it studded the Russian lands with cupolas, littered it with ikons, stifled it with priests. Not the Gothic that pressed in from Sweden with Rurik and from Germany with the Romanovs. Not the liberalism of France and England, despite Catherine and Peter. Now, the Communist Revolution has come in—intricate synthesis in its Russian form of all of these. It has something of Islam, something of the Greek Church, something of Gothic mysticism, of German romanticism, of the rationalism of France, of the mechanolatry of England. It is a world-force, the first to take root and form in Russia: the first that may spring—if the world-climate ripens for it—from Russian seed and soil into world-flower.

Of Russia's past formlessness in culture, the Volga that winds from the Baltic to the Caspian, between two continents, is the perfect symbol. And it is the perfect scene (Lenin was born on the Volga) of the struggle of the inchoate land to grow culturally ordered. On the Volga rise heroic factories of the Five-year Plan—from Nizhni Novgorod to Stalingrad. On the Volga I am watching the even more historic movement of the muzhik from his individualistic farm to the proletarian collective.

Tatar Kazan is the Volga's heart. As I stand on its first street where it meets the river that joins it to all the Union, I have within my eyes the crude drama of Russia's revolutionary will from confusion into order. The street is unpaved and the mud is thick. But there is a track: here a string of freight-cars, there a tiny trolley that will carry us (if it does not break down) to Kazan centre. The houses, wood and brick, are a disjointed gallery of booths, co-operatives, longshoremen's quarters, soviet offices. They face every way in the mud, behind them is swamp and all about them a huge human swarming.

Here are long Tatars with Mongol eyes and Russian beards, wearing the turban of Islam. Jews, reeking with prayer, who have lost their trade and whose children have disowned them. Communist youth with pale faces and ruthless lips, making plans *en place* for the reorganization of the harbor. Women mechanics in black uniforms, who have left their children in the state school twenty versts up the river and visit them every sixth day—the Russian "sunday." A gang of convicts, double-file, in dirty yellow, move down the street to their barracks. They have been laying tracks. No guard walks with them. Many of them are lads who once roamed the countryside in packs, slashing and stealing—the dreaded *bezprizorniy,* waifs of Revolution. Communism has reclaimed them, and set them at work on their honor. They pass a single file of workers waiting in line at a co-operative for bread. They pass a crowd circled about a gipsy—a huge black fellow with flaming mustachios who at the instant is swallowing a sword. They move slower, so as to see the curved blade sink into the man's throat and be drawn out, clean and bloodless. They swing along past a wide wood structure on whose porch a score of children play with blocks and dolls. Many of these are almost too large to be called children: all of them play dully and look with idiot eyes at their white-aproned nurses.

The convicts at last reach a pier where a throng of muzhiks with bundles on their backs are trying to clamber over a Ford that blocks the gangway to the boat. The car is jammed, the score of sailors helplessly shove at it. But the muzhiks do not realize that the boat cannot leave until the car is on board: they fight with the sailors, they swarm over the Ford, fouling its upholstery, scratching its varnish. A mass of timber is strewn disordered in the mud. It has come from the Siberian forests, and is destined for the Soviet House that rises, half-finished (its lower floor in use, its upper ones still skeletal) across the street from the boat. A man in puttees and a black blouse sights the gang of convicts from his office window, rushes out, and speaks to the first pair. A few words are exchanged; then the thirty boys in prison yellow fall to and pile the lumber in neat rows before the unfinished building. The black-bloused man has not waited to supervise them; he has left for his dinner. No one thanks the convicts; they fall in line and proceed to their own meal.

Across the river lies a cloud steel-black with storm, and huge on the horizon. The sun, long hidden, suddenly burns through. The cloud is gashed with blood. A new day half iron and half flame pours upon Kazan. Russia's chaos and Russia's will for order take on the day's colors.

The boat was getting to be more and more crowded. It was a graceful vessel, once the pride of the Tsar's river service. Its long hull had the trim lines in which even the heaviest barge we passed was not wholly lacking. The saloon and music rooms were fitted in summery birch with cool panels and high ceilings. On the central hall, a number of cabins opened; this was the "soft" part of the steamer and was filled by army officers, skilled mechanics, GPU men and a miscellany of women with their children. The "hard" passengers soon overflowed the under decks, the hold, all available dark corners. Muzhik women began to camp on the companionway; when I went down to the kitchen to get hot water, I had to step with care across the children. From the companionway they spread to the main hall, to the upper deck, to the music room. Outside my cabin, a quiet mother disposed her three babies in a rug: I felt ashamed of my bed, as I heard them breathe and stir at night. The whole ship was soon overwhelmed by the "hard" travelling peasants. We rode low and slow in the yellow water, losing time as we proceeded.

The *Raskolnikov* was becoming an epitome of the Union. Every class was here of this new world aiming toward classlessness: the new aristocrat, a young Communist laborer travelling "soft" on a vacation to Astrakhan and points south; the new *bourzhui,* a Soviet inspector bound for Saratov; the soldier, the mechanic, the proletarianized peasant, the unregenerate muzhik. Even the Russian navy was represented, by a pilot from the Baltic— a young blond husky with thick lips and stony eyes. He carried his own eggs, meat, caviar and vodka. His rosy cheeks grew flushed, and remained so. At first he sat at table with a man whom I spotted as GPU, a stout fellow with clever sensitive eyes and a weak mouth. Then a woman joined them. She gave her little girl into the care of Ilyena (who had so much to do that one more task was nothing); and herself to the delight of being courted. She was a heavy woman whose full rondures bespoke a feline nature. She was dressed in a long black skirt, for she had learned that skirts were lengthening in Paris. Her jacket was too small for her bust and without relation to her skirt. She had small soft hands and large feet. She laughed and drank with her two men all day, and worked assiduously on the problem of whom she should sleep with at night. Abruptly, she chose the GPU man,—perhaps symbolically since the GPU is indeed more powerful than all the other forces of the Union. Any woman of her type, in Europe, would have deferred her choice, or at least kept it secret until the end of the journey. But flirtatiousness and the deliberate sexual game are rare in Russia. These two men wanted her body, and her body wanted a man. She made her choice as honestly and swiftly as she could. The disdained pilot exhausted his vodka. His dull eyes glowered with angry fire, as he rolled up and down the deck, hunting another woman.

Then the ship's food gave out. Ilyena, moist and weary but still smiling, told us that there was plenty of water for our tea; and we could get caviar and apples. Also, there was kasha—a delicious buckwheat gruel, but without butter or milk to soften it, and plenty of coarse black bread. My stomach is more conservative than either my mind or my emotions. It refused persistently to digest that bread, despite my fruitful analogues between its flavor and the flavor of Russian life. I settled down to a regime of caviar and tea; and I did not like it.

Caviar for breakfast is not so good; and caviar that has grown warm and rancid is a nuisance. We had to pay for all our food, of course; and the price of those half-rotten sturgeon eggs on the Volga was even more exorbitant than the same dainty, properly iced, at the Crillon. Yet I saved money—in the long run. For I am sick of caviar; I shall never buy caviar again.

One evening, after we had left Samara, a crowd of us were in the music room. The GPU man shouted revolutionary songs, while his lady at the piano turned her lush body toward him. A huge man with the head of a horse sang old folk songs. I had talked with him, and noted in him the typical Russian peasant paradox of intellectual dullness and exquisite finesse. Where could not this sensibility of nerves lead his coarse body? to what vistas could it not incite his mind? He had become a city man, a Communist metal worker. And he sang the plaints of his muzhik forebears in a voice warm, clear, gentle as twilight on the summer steppe. The music of the Revolution, I learned, was the old folk music. Only its pace had been quickened, its contours hardened and crowded to sharper intervals, its rhythms edged from curve to angle.

Here was the deepest proof—music and folk dance do not lie—that the Communist Revolution is Russian. A natural process is crystallizing the chaos of the land into a world of time and factories and factory farms. Yet deep in the song which the Red Army shouts as it marches through the industrial city is the voice of the muzhik. Uttering the new song, is the old tongue; thinking it, is the ancestral muzhik head.

A feeling of strangeness gradually won me, and I went out on deck. The night was humid. The shore was a darker black within the darkness. On shore was a light, and it was not moving! Yet our engine throbbed at its customary pace. What could that mean? I leaned overboard. The shore light was not moving, because we were not moving. The racing engine told the story: we were grounded!

I returned to the music room and whispered my news to the GPU man. He smiled at me. Every Russian in that room had known for a couple of hours what I had just discovered.

"What are we going to do?" I asked the navy pilot.

The folly of my question made him forget his troubles.

"What indeed?" he laughed. "We will drink vodka, we will go to bed, we will even go to sleep —since we must go to bed alone! We will awake."

The entire ship was aware we were grounded. Only I, the American, was in the least concerned. After all, to be stuck in the Volga sands is important only for him who lives by the watch, who wants regular meals at regular hours—important only for us barbarians of the machine. I felt acutely the limitations of my western training. Here we are grounded. Some time or another, a boat will come along and push us free. There is at least a month before the Volga freezes. Meanwhile, a pause has come upon us: a warm pause in which women and men come close, singing, drinking, sleeping. Only I am moved—by a habit—to leap from this pause, to deny its richness.

That night a great peace fell upon the boat. We were lifted out of time; we were poised sweetly in an essential moment that was neither space nor time. As on the pier of Nizhni Novgorod with the waiting muzhiks, I tasted the substance of a people. Men and women sat motionless on deck, children slumbered, couples moved close together in the shadows, song drifted down the river, and the mild waves resounded music. Slowly, sweetly, fertilely, we swung in the equipoise of life . . . together. And I knew in that moment the essential health of what was happening in Russia. A fresh spirit was born, and was whole. Time might twist it, inadequate ideas might destroy it, the outer world might choke it. *Now,* this life is healthy, as a babe is healthy.

In the dawn two tug boats reached us from Samara. Silently, they nosed into our flank and pushed us to deep water.

It occurred to me that I had never seen the captain. Surely the boat—even in the proletarian dictatorship—must have a captain! In the pilot room, there were always a couple of sailors in blouses, smoking, chatting, perhaps occasionally steering. Were they and Ilyena—who was maître d'hôtel, cabin and dining steward, purser, nurse—the ship's whole crew? Carol said:

"I've found the Captain's wife, so there must be a Captain."

She was a little woman with motherly eyes. I had noticed her as she spoke soothingly to the peasants, or held a babe. Always, when I passed her, she had smiled at me. Now, I realized it had been the smile of a hostess at a party rather too large for personal introductions (which are not "done" at any rate in the Soviet Union). She smiled still more broadly at Carol's question.

"Oh, yes," she said, "there is a captain."

"Is he on board?"

"Oh, yes, he is on board. You have probably seen him. He does not wear his uniform. You see, the ship is very crowded, and the food is very scarce. The Captain is afraid—if he wore his uniform—the peasants might find him and throw him into the water."

5

Had I stayed in Russia long enough I should have learned the language as a child learns its mother tongue: directly by ear without benefit of the reading eye. I could already understand many spoken words with the atmospheric aid of the speaker's mood and inflection. But my poor tongue could not repeat these words. I was like a babe apprehending dimly a fragment of what is said and not yet ready to speak. Synchronously, I was like a boy of six just learning his letters. Every printed sign I automatically spelled to myself and then spoke aloud—eagerly awaiting Carol's approval of my pronunciation. On the river, my one chance to spell was given by the boats that constantly passed us; every boat had its name in decorative letters on the box of its side wheel or under its stern. We were approaching Saratov. A rakish steamer swept up the river. It was painted white, with red-shuttered cabins and brass rails, and a smartly tilted stack. I found:

ЖОН РИД

"Zh-o-n R-i-d," I spelled aloud. "What does that mean, Carol?"

"John Reed," she said.

We are ready to land, having paid and embraced Ilyena. A "hard" traveller, who is landing also and who has bunked in the dining saloon, stands at our side, our bags and blankets strapped to his giant shoulders. He is a proletarianized muzhik, bound for a factory in Saratov. He nods when Carol names John Reed. He knows him. I also knew him. And I see him again, the year 1917, the place New York. He is a big boy, although he would be dwarfed beside this peasant. His cheeks are bland, his eyes have an almost girlish candor which the mouth belies, thin and resolute. There has been a meeting in the Bronx against President Wilson's draft law. Emma Goldman has spoken. We pour into the street, singing the International. The police advance on us, and we scatter like sheep, our song shredding and fading. Jack stands with me under the Third Avenue "L." He is furious and contemptuous.

"They're afraid of the policemen's club," he says. "Some day they'll get hit in spite of themselves. Then they'll learn it don't hurt so much. Then we'll be ready for the Revolution."

Troubadour Jack Reed, seeking his distant princess the world over—Mexico, Serbia, Russia: his loved lady Revolution. I had a feeling half of contempt for Jack in 1917. We had argued, and I did not admire his logic. He had sent stories to the magazine I edited, and I did not too greatly admire his stories. I loved the playboy, the troubadour. Reed seemed to me a seeker of romance: he seemed to me unreal, both in his values and his methods. But he had gone to Russia, worked with Lenin, helped in the October Revolution. Was that real? He had died for the Revolution. His tomb stood under the Kremlin wall in Moscow. Yes: he had been real enough in 1917. Quite as real as the philosophic radical who argued with him. He had been so real that he is a legend and a hero six thousand miles from his home. So real that Russian boats are called for him; that muzhiks nod at his name. So real that he has become a symbol. To the Soviet Union he is the symbol of American good will—the real America of brotherhood beneath the dismal claque of Business. And who shall say this America is not real? To me also Jack Reed at last is real, because to me also he is a symbol. Through him, I poignantly know that this Russian scene is bound to my own life. I am at home in Russia, as much at home as I was in 1917 under the Bronx "L." Russia has become a theatre of the spirit: a place where human will, human values, are incarnate. It no longer seems strange that an illiterate peasant on the Volga in 1932 should know John Reed of Harvard. Like Reed himself, Russia with its chaos and its tragic search for human wholeness is a symbol. A symbol in flesh and blood, a symbol so profound that all the vast Russian lands from Minsk to the Pacific are insignificant within it. It is a symbol so immediate to my modern mind that in this town on the Volga, where I and my blood have never been, I feel at home.

6

Saratov made me think of Chekhov. The town is stagnant. When there is wind only the dust blows, and when there is rain there is only the mud. The wide residential streets are sodden and sad. Behind their wood fences, the houses rot with shutters drawn. But if you come close, you will find doors gently carved, windows with fair tooling, in the rank weed of the garden a lyric fountain. Saratov is like an ancient cherry orchard whose moldering trees still glow with blossoms.

Chekhov is an alien artist in the Soviet Union. His souls floundering in the social swamps of the late Tsars have been swept away by the revolutionary current; and in the main streets of Saratov, the Leninskaya and the Nikolskaya, I feel the pulsant rising of a life that will destroy Chekhovian Saratov—and all the similar towns phosphorescently decaying in Russia.

As we approached the station, the pulse beat higher. The life of the Union flows through arteries of railroads. The station throbbed with human charge. And the train for Moscow stood gorged with travellers, both hard and soft. Not a place for us. We rushed to the GPU. The young officer—hard mouth, cropped hair, a Jesuit's brow and gentle eyes—bent his long head over our passports. He smoked a few American cigarettes, and then he scribbled for us the magic *bumaga*—the slip of paper that does miracles in Russia. In this case, when we presented it to the *notchalnik stanzi* it created two berths for us, in a soft compartment.

"We had better buy food," said Carol. "It's twenty hours to Moscow, you know. Even if we're on time."

"And the train is already an hour late in starting."

My hunger was only for Moscow. It was so long since my stomach had known anything more substantial than tea and caviar that it had forgotten to be hungry.

"Come along," insisted Carol, like a good housewife. "One eats when one can, you know."

We worked our way through an army of women bivouacked on the station floor with children, samovars and household goods spread out like barricades. We reached the buffet counter. We bought a can of milk, two loaves of comparatively pale bread, two paper plates of salad, cucumbers, and a yard of sausage. We paid what a fine dinner with *Liebfraumilch* would have cost us at the Adlon in Berlin. Then we went to our compartment.

There is something about a Russian train standing at a station, that thrills. You feel the journey's adventure. The little locomotive is human: it represents the dogged will of little man to pull great loads great distances. The dingy cars are human, they have been lived in. Long hours and days (there are few short hauls in Russia) the hard benches have been warmed by families who have eaten and slept in them, argued and prayed, nursed babes and begot new ones. The station itself—the open platform, the stockade of unpainted wood under the sky—is a symbol of Russia's plains whose vastness the little caravan is ready to traverse. It is the immediate human, the want of stereotype, that makes Russia so exciting. There are no separate things in Russia, no separate persons. Every object, however small, is linked, by the consciousness of him who made it or who uses it, with life itself. Therefore it is wholly human; which means that it is dramatic. And every person is in full flowing action with the folk about him. Therefore, he is vital—with the whole vitality of Russia. What bores is the thing or the instant that stands alone: that does not draw us by contact with it into communion with ourselves and our world. There is nothing boring in Russia, because there is nothing detached.

Wherever one is, one is in contact with all. That is why Russian fiction has been the best in the world.[1] And that is why Russia logically adopts a Communist religion.

But how can there be, in Russia, both continuity and chaos? The continuity is of the flesh and of the spirit: it is both animal and mystic. It links the people like creatures of a herd; and it exalts the persons—a Tolstoi, an Alyosha—into ecstatic bonds with God: the bonds of art and of religion. The chaos is *social*. It has been manifest in every phase of Russian business, politics, economics. The Revolution, in one aspect, is Russia's national need to transpose the strength of continuity from the instinctive and emotive realms where it has long prevailed, into regions of the conscious mind where it can organize the people. To make of community and continuity an active principle for personal ethics and a modern social order. To change wholeness from a *feeling* into a *method* of intelligence and will.

Two young women shared our compartment with us. Before I came to Russia, the expectation of this kind of freedom had sent my mind on wild imaginings. But the reality of Russia is so intense

[1] I do not mean that all the greatest novelists have been Russian —far from it. But nowhere else, in the nineteenth century, was the level of fiction so high.

that almost immediately it conquers the old habits of thought: conventions of the West in the new light become fantastic. There is nothing naturally strange, for a man, in sleeping with women in a tightly shut compartment. And he discovers that it is not strange. The women lie in their berths with their bodies covered; and so does he. If he wants to look at them, there is nothing to stop him. The night has dignity, reserve, and a subtle tenderness of feeling as between comrades. Sexual passion, in the *human* culture toward which Russia aspires, does not depend on accident . . . because it is never suppressed. If a man and a woman want each other, they do not wait for a fortuity so absurd as a night on a train, to bring them close. If desire does not deeply move them, the fact of their sleeping together on a train will mean nothing.

The one girl was an engineer stationed in a cotton mill at Shakmatova. Three days before, the factory Soviet had granted her a vacation. "It's the first I've had in three years." And she was going to spend it in Moscow. "I'm not going to think about spindles for three whole weeks," she said. "In the mornings, I'm going to the Lenin Institute. I want to know how he lived all the years before the Revolution. Afternoons, I shall play tennis—if it isn't too cold."

She was not pretty; her nose and her features were too large and her eyes were too small, and her skin was coarse. But her body was alive in the drab clothes.

"Do you know with whom you are going to play tennis?"

"Yes, I know," she replied softly.

The second girl was radiant and tall. Her hempen braids coiled above a brow delicate as a child's; but her mouth was ripe and strong. In a cream-colored smock, worn and outgrown, her breasts stood forth with candor, and her throat throbbed as she breathed. She was going to Moscow as a delegate of the Komsomol—the Youth's Communist Party. She worked in a grain elevator in Saratov, earning sixty roubles a month; and her name was Natacha.

I asked the older girl if she was a Party member. When she answered No, Natacha looked at her with eyes deliberately forbearing, as if to say: "I am making an effort to be tolerant, not to judge, not to seem superior." It was plain that Natacha was a Communist fanatic.

An army man was smoking in the corridor outside our open door. Seeing three young women with one old man, he came in and sat down. He had a small close-shaven head and piercing eyes. The muscles of his torso bulged rhythmically in his drab uniform. He was aware of the girls, but he spoke only to me. He listened to Carol who served as my interpreter, impatiently as if she barred his immediate contact with this American whom he was eager to question.

What was my work in the U. S. A.? How much did I earn? What was I doing in the Soviet Union? What was I going to say when I got home? How did the western countries feel about the Union? Was there danger of war? And when I answered: Yes, of course, there was danger of war on the U. S. S. R., I found in his soldier eyes the same pain, the same dark flash of terror and of pity which every Russian had revealed to me when the prospect of having to give up the Soviet peace and the Plan, in order to fight, was put before him. . . . Was I a Communist? No. But I believed in the universal need of social revolution? What, then, *was* I?

I tried to explain my reasons, ideological and technical, for not joining any party. He shook his head.

"If you believe in the Revolution, you must be a Communist," he said. "Here in Russia it would not be necessary. We have started on our way, and the non-Communists must be with us. But in the Capitalist countries, either you are for the Revolution or you are against it. Which means: either you are a Communist or a bourgeois. If you think you have ideological reasons for not joining the Party, that means that you have bourgeois ideals. Communism has the truth: in history, in art, in science. It has the method for abolishing the classes, and for directing man's future. If you don't accept these truths, you are against the future: you are bound by the bourgeois past. And that means you must be liquidated, like the past." Here the good soldier drew his hand across his throat, in order to show what must happen to my head.

I tried to explain to him that the method of creating the Revolutionary future might be different in my country—since our past was different. He answered:

"There is nothing Russian about Communist truths. Russia no longer exists. Stalin is not a Russian, Marx was not a Russian, nor is Litvinov a Russian. Communism will unlock the brotherhood of man with the same key in China, in Africa and in America. The truth is the truth. . . ."

As he sat there smoking, warmly aware of the three women, talking only to me, I knew that I had before me a happy man. He had found the Truth, and there was room in it for all his life—feeling and action. Like millions of others, this soldier had been born in Russia's formless plain, which in Tsarist days gave two directions to his need of order: the animal sleep of herd-life and sense-indulgence or the unearthly peace of the Saints. But now he had a truth that kept him close to earth and that deployed all his dreams; that made him wholly human and that moved him to merge his will in an ideal beyond the person. A happy man.

At the next stop I rushed out with a hundred other passengers to the station faucet of *kipyetok* —boiling water. As the train lurched on into the Russian night we made tea and broke bread and ate sausage. The open window let in clouds of dust, so we shut it tight. The compartment was dirty with scraps of food, spilled water, moist soot: clothing and bags lay indiscriminate on the floor and bench of our compartment, and the air was thick with cigarettes. The soldier kept on talking. Now Natacha joined with contributions of her own.

The conductress called for our tickets and remained to listen. She was a short woman in a dark gray jumper that came down to her knees. Her bandy legs were cased in cotton stockings, but her bare arms were finely molded. She leaned on the door sill, and drank in the truths of the soldier and of Natacha—her truths also, and more glorious and sustaining every blesséd time she heard them.

Suddenly she remembered her duties. She shoved us all into the corridor, and prepared to spread sheet and blanket on each of the four berths. We drew into a station where there was a half hour's stop. Carol, the girl engineer and the soldier, went out to buy cakes. The conductress completed her task, and left Natacha and me alone in the compartment.

Unlike the girl engineer, Natacha knew no word of any language except Russian. Neither she nor I could place the common barrier of words against the radiance of her beauty full upon me. There was nothing to do, but sit on the bed and look at her and receive the gaze of her candid eyes on mine. I knew I could not touch her. Her physical fairness was no wine in a glass, to sip or to drain. Her beauty was herself. Her unquestioning faith in the Communist religion, her womanhood which also she unquestioning accepted, were integral of her beauty. Had we sat together all that night, I should have wanted not to touch her. To have caressed Natacha must have been to take all of her: not alone the fragrant body and the heart with its clear-singing need of a mate to cleave by her and give her children, but as well the mind with its convictions. Her tender form was but the outward chalice of the stern Communist flower.

We sat and smiled into each other's eyes. And I

knew that she knew what I was feeling. And I knew that she knew the poignance of my being in her world, and what I should carry away with me. My being deep in Russia on this train that was bearing us to Moscow, was alive with fragrance like the body of this girl. My presence here, and her own, we possessed together.

Carol and the engineer returned. The train plunged into the night that lay between us and Moscow. Carol and the engineer were to have the lower berths. Natacha and I clambered into the two upper ones. I put out the light.

III

MOSCOW

MOSCOW

We stand under the huge red buildings of the
Electrozavod. Within are twenty-five thousand
workers, and there is a constant flow of them, in
and out the gate. This is one of the great plants of
Moscow; it manufactures every electrical need
from bulbs to dynamos. I presume it is not typical,
since it exceeded its quota of production under the
Five-year Plan in less than three. But it is archetypical. Inside the gates is a new world. The brick
walls flare out, making a number of tall and narrow streets. High up is a loud-speaker: it rever-
berates incessant exhortation to the men and women: the metallic words of propaganda roll down
the streets, bound from the stone pavements, vol-
ley from wall to wall. The men move with em-
phasis, rhythmical like the phrases of the loud-
speaker. Their faces are set; they move in an atmosphere of crisis. This is indeed an army and a
war. The buildings are grim like war; the beat of
the machines inside the walls, the delicate vibra-
tions of myriad hands and feet, merge into a
mighty pulse that catches all the buildings: the

works throb rhythmic and incessant like a battery in battle. But this war is not death.

The engineer who is to guide us through the works is a pure proletarian Russian. His pock-marked face is gentle, the eyes cast warmth over its pallor. We stand in a vast dark hall where the parts of dynamos are welded. The men work intensely, yet with a quiet reserve. They have no mechanical ease like the operatives in an American plant: they appear to be working more with their minds than with their hands, and more with their spirit than with their minds. They resist giving us attention as we pass. And when the engineer stops a group of them, in order that we may ask them questions, they seem to emerge from a distant realm . . . like poets suddenly recalled into the surface of a prosaic world.

These proletarians are, after all, the children of muzhiks. I have seen them work their soil, so rapt in the service of the plow that they did not look up although a strange car passed them. Whether these men will keep on working their machines in the same spirit, as if they were cultivating or composing, whether their way is as efficient as the American's who divides his hand from his soul, making his hand part of the machine it serves rather than of his mind and spirit, are unanswered questions.

There were women working everywhere; even in the heavy sectors their masked faces gleamed amid the clang of iron and the blare of flame. In certain places where the work is delicate, like the piecing together of the parts of the bulb, there were more women than men. Everywhere was the same emotion. The grim set mouths, the eyes intent on conscious application, the physical fervor —as of boys and girls giving themselves to a game on which their lives depended.

I have been in factories in many parts of the world: I have always been depressed, for I have felt that the workers were either unhappy or too dead to know that their humanity was suffering. They were bent to a task that cut them off from self. Here are happy workers, because here are whole men and women. Although their individual job be a single motion endlessly repeated, although they stand enslaved for hours to the turn of a wheel which they must feed and feed—yet in these dismal halls there is a whole humanity. Dream, thought, love, collaborate in the tedious business of making electric parts, since these toilers are not working for a boss—not even for a living: the least of them knows that he is making a Worker's Union, that he is creating a world.

Up two dingy flights, we came to the offices. The director stands before a long table of unpainted pine at which men like himself sit to meet the factory problems. He is dressed in a black blouse and wears puttees. His face is long and gaunt; his mouth hard, his eyes brilliant. He does not like to be bothered by visitors; he resents having to detail engineers to show them through the plant: every visit, he knows, is a loss in man-hours. He looks at me, trying hard to be courteous, and asks me to be seated. I tell him these thoughts I have read in his eyes. Then he smiles. Such visits as mine, I tell him, are useful, after all. It is important for the world to know that factory workers can be happy. Such plants as this one he directs are not making merely electric lights for U. S. S. R.: they have a product of another kind, light of another kind, made for export.

"Yes," he says severely, "we are aware of our responsibility to the world. We know we are working for the world. It is because we are aware of this," now he smiles warmly, "that we allow ourselves to be pestered."

This man has a good head and a strong will. I feel in him a clarity of mental process, similar to that of good executives in the United States. His mind is simple and immediate. Yet he is utterly different from the American magnate risen, like himself, from the ranks. There is in this Russian an essential *innocence*. He is ruthless, but he is *clean.* Life has not twisted him from his original humanity; his rise has not hypertrophied some single parts of him at the expense of the whole. There may be factory heads in the capitalist countries with more brains and more imagination than this proletarian Russian. But insofar as they are magnates, one and all, the capitalists have had to think of personal gain in terms of worsting rivals and of exploiting men. Being primarily humans and not beasts, they have had to reconcile their daily act of downing others with their decency, by hiding the true nature of their acts from themselves. The taint of rationalization about "service" and of insincerity concerning their real motives, is in the best of them. This man, through no virtue of his own but by grace of a system ideologically pure, is innocent. He has had no thought of money in personal terms; he has had no thought even of profit or of power, save in terms of Russia and the workers' world.

I make no prophecy for the future: there'll be time for such speculations when I have left the Union. It may be that the corruption of personal power will find its way into the industrial leadership of U. S. S. R. There are, alas! signs of it, already, in the political world. A new falsehood, as hideous as ours, may make havoc in this world. But the rationalized death which a culture of personal aggrandizement has spread like a miasma throughout the Christian lands was not upon this man. I felt in him the heart of a still sound human wholeness.

"There are a number of detailed questions I'd like to ask," I finally said, "and it's not you I should be bothering to answer them."

The director nodded and spoke a few words with my interpreter. We shook hands and I went into another office. Newspapers mimeographed in several languages were posted on the walls; and portraits of "shock brigaders"—the best workers whose reward is concrete, consisting of higher pay, better vacations, and exclusive purchase privileges at some of the stores. On another wall were the crayoned faces of "slackers"—the men and women who were not doing their share. They received no punishment except this moral one— and the additional disgrace of being paid at the "black wicket," a booth set up for them beside the others, in the cashier's office.

A young man joined us. He was the head of the Workers' Committee on Inventions. He led us into a little room with an American desk, three kitchen stools and the four walls crowded with statistical charts. He sat down at the desk and looked me in the eye.

"I have been instructed to answer your questions about the factory work. I think it would be best if you give me a number of questions at once; then I can arrange my answers economically. Of course, you can add further ones. Please proceed."

My interpreter, a brainy fellow from an academy of languages wearing an Esperanto button, detailed my questions; the worker's face grew sharp with concentration. I could see that his health was frail; doubtless in the years of his childhood—the terrible years of War and Civil War—there had been many months when bread was scarce. His mouth and eyes and brow revealed a sensitive man: all his life he had worked with his hands, yet he was closer to the artist than to the western factory worker. His eyes burned with an ascetic flame, and his warm lips were hardened by discipline. He might have been a saintly artisan in some medieval convent, who has turned his love of color and of music to the building of an impersonal heaven.

My interpreter stopped; there was a long pause in which without discomfort the young man assembled his answers in his mind. Then he spoke, giving figures and details, soberly, in a monotone that sounded almost like a prayer. I learned what I wanted to know of the piece-work pay, of the invention-rewards, of the relation between the workers and their committees, between the factory and the trade unions and the Politburo.

"Is there not danger," I said at last, "to your Communist ideal? 'From each according to his ability, to each according to his need'—has always seemed to me the golden rule of socialism: the very essence of a Communist world, in which value and human rivalry are lifted from the physical plane of possession and power. Yet here you are, remunerating inventions with money, paying superior sums of money to the more capable men. Here you are, planning your new hierarchy of merit by the old hated symbol of *money*. Even in your collective farms, the money measure of merit has been re-introduced! I am worried, I confess. It almost seems as if you were fighting the old order by infecting yourselves with the disease which rotted it."

He answered: "I was instructed, tovarishtch, to inform you about the working details of the factory. To discuss socialist theory with you is not my commission, and not my province. But as an individual, I will try to answer your objections. . . .

"The Soviet Union is not yet Communist. We are in the transition stage of the proletarian dictatorship. Since the world Revolution is still to come, we are in a state of war with the surrounding countries. Internally and externally, we have an emergency situation to which the final abolition of classes, here and abroad, will put an end. Very well. To meet this temporary emergency, we must induce the men we have—men brought up in a capitalist world, men still open to capitalist ideas —to speed up our production. We must do this by any means that will convince them—even by individualistic rewards. We cannot afford to wait. We *must* have machines in order to speed the historic process. But meantime, our children are being brought up with pure Communist values. They are being taught to work collectively, and for collective ends. They are being taught to despise all personal rewards. While they grow in their Communist habits, we are proceeding to wipe out the old capitalist structure. Our children will inherit a classless world, in which the very idea of monetary reward will be absurd."

"You mean that the standard by which your young people are being taught to live will be stronger than the example they see before them: the example of shock brigaders and bureaucrats getting special pay for their work?"

He nodded.

"But when," I asked, hoping to be convinced, "when has education not been according to an ideal superior to the practiced way of life? And when has the ideal prevailed against a reality which belied it?"

He did not answer, but he smiled at my small faith—I who was comparing the Soviet future with any past the world had ever seen.

"The good ideals of the old cultures," my interpreter suggested, "were not based on the reality of mankind: they were absolute denials of reality; they were rationalizations of a privileged class. They were, indeed, the rationalized accomplices of the bad reality outside."

"Very well," I said, "I agree. The good ideals of all past education were dualistic—and hence doomed. I agree. They did not apply to life as it was ordered. But is there not a kindred danger in the class of better-paid men to-day in the Soviet Union? With their greater ability might they not erect a new hierarchy, a new bourgeoisie; might they not somehow manage to perpetuate their own privileges (which they *personally* deserve) for the sake of their wives and friends and children? And if that comes, won't they begin to teach a new dualism in the schools which they will control, in order to rationalize their superior place?"

"This can never be," the young man answered,

quietly, "in a Union where every instrument of education and of art heaps constant contempt on the idea of personal privilege and personal possession."

"Did Christianity approve," I countered, "of personal privilege and personal possession?"

"Christianity," replied the worker, "encouraged the idea of personal privilege and possession by its idea of a heaven to be *personally* achieved. And Christianity did nothing to fight personal privilege and possession here on earth, and it condoned the classes which perpetuated them. Moreover, the lust for goods and power—here or hereafter—is born of poverty and fear. Poverty and fear have no place in a Communist world. Therefore, the lust will go. Indeed, it is going already."

We went down again into the inner factory streets. The loud-speaker volleyed from wall to wall. The workers streamed incessantly. We passed dull blocks of dwellers' houses, and entered a huge factory kitchen. The meal was ample and well cooked, one of the best I had had in Russia. And the kvass—essence of Russia's bread—was delicious.

All day I wandered in and out of the red buildings. I sat in the Lenin corner, chatting with tired girls who had come for a cigarette and a glass of tea; I stood by machines that kept strong men in a perpetual wracking motion. Never was I outside the rhythm of comrades bent to their individual tasks but sustained by the knowledge of their crucial part in a great human whole.

2

The factory throbs in Moscow like a young heart in an old body—a heart that is bursting the body. Muscovite Moscow burned when Napoleon entered it; but the rebuilt city regathered its ancestral form since its life had not changed. It was still the city of the thousand nobles, the thousand merchants, and the horde of serfs who, as the nineteenth century waned, became the proletariat of the "world's largest village."

A city of disorder. The nobles lived carelessly on the wealth sent from their lands by dishonest stewards. The merchants lived barbarously on the huge toll they took of goods passing between the Black and the White Seas. Neither class was concerned with the life of the nether mass, the toilers and servants, so long as they obeyed orders and begot new slaves. The streets reflected this indifference. They were dark, unpaved, a huddled disarray of festering houses beneath the flaunt of the churches whose gold domes hoarded all the sun. And to-day, Moscow still bespeaks this past. Its common architecture is a chaos without dignity or power. Its common streets—the perouloks—are still the streets of a degraded folk; and the squares with their dingy trees and crumbling mansions are still the homes of masters degraded by their degradation of their brothers.

In its general form, Moscow is remarkably like Paris. Here were towns in the north centre of a medieval country unified by trade routes. Here were rivers, the Seine and the Moskva with its outlet (the Volga), making the whole land accessible. At Moscow, the river makes a sharp double turn like the Seine at Paris; and in the water-enclosed land there was the similar logical seat for a fortress. What became the Cité in Paris (with Notre Dame) is the high Moscow Kremlin. And the walled section about the Cité, concentric with the Seine, whose remnants to-day are the Portes Saint Martin and Saint Denis and whose placement is marked by the interior boulevards, becomes in Moscow the walled Kitai Gorod and Byely Gorod—the "Chinese" and "White" cities. Moscow also grew concentrically from its fortress heart (which was both secular and sacred) in a number of sweeping semi-circles roughly traced by boulevards. Moscow also, as it grew, leaped its river on bridges, and in the last century broke its river form by spreading into industrial suburbs whose distinction from the old town was soon lost, like the distinction of the *faubourgs* beyond ancestral Paris.

But the contrast between the two towns is more revealing than the structural kinship which marks the usual growth of river-fastnesses in Europe. Paris in its circlings from the Cité remains organic. The traits of the centre with its palaces, churches, squares, are variedly repeated throughout the town. The city is *one;* substantially, even qualitatively, there is no break from the old Ile-Saint-Louis to the farthest slope of Montmartre: there is only organic progression (or deterioration which is a kind of progression) in style as in the years with which the town grew. Not so Moscow. The theocratic Kremlin bristles with palace and church. Beyond its walls on the embankment and on the central squares, the magnificence continues: there is height, there is generous space. At once, thereafter, come congestion and darkness within the walls of the old merchant town. And beyond these walls, Moscow is a sprawling village. The houses of the urbanized serfs are low, the streets dawdle, the squares are misshapen and humble. Even the three circles of concentric boulevards do not give order, for the buildings are architectural chaos and the parked promenades are crowded with a folk still essentially rustic. Humble

Moscow looks more like a fair at Nizhni Novgorod than like a metropolitan city.

Gradually, of course, the new heart that glows in the factories all over Russia is transforming this old Moscow. The streets that radiate from the Red Square and Sverdlov Square to the first system of boulevards are smooth with asphalt; new buildings bring symmetry—great stores, post offices, lodgings for Soviet officials, trade-union quarters or the grim fastness of the GPU. They gleam in fresh cement, they parade in the sheer angles and cubes of an architecture borrowed from Holland, against the prevalent litter of the old town. In my brief time in Moscow, I saw an entire square razed of its convents and musty mansions; doubtless to-day some new abstraction of industrial power stands where the Byzantine incense used to curl to heaven.

But the bulk of the city is still old Moscow. As it loses sight of the Kremlin towers, it moves with ease into the fields surrounding. And the city is closer in feeling to the fields than to the gemmed geometry of Saint Basil's or the drab geometry of the new Soviet buildings.

They are verdant meadows. Through the long winter they shrewdly guard their redolence beneath the snows; and with the returning sun they sing with vigor. They are fields whose strength is so sure that it is gentle. They rise in quiet cadence, they flame into sudden copses of birch, they subside into lawns with mellow izbas. The fields about Moscow give a fertile flavor to the darkest peroulok, sweeten the toil of its poor, come with warm magic to the factories.

Field and workshop must breathe together; to the one must come human order, to the second, nature. Between them, field and factory will give birth to the *body* of Revolution. And Moscow heralds this consummation. That is why, as against Leningrad with its bleak hinterland, Moscow of the fertile fields is the capital of Soviet Russia.

3

One sunny afternoon, I was riding through the fields in a brand-new Ford. At the wheel was its owner, a famous Russian novelist, who had earned dollars with translations of his books, thus becoming one of the richest men of the Union. Writers may sell their work abroad, may even go abroad to drum up trade, provided they return in due time with the *valuta*. Even the authors who remain at home and whose work is not translated can prosper; the correct kind of word is well paid by the Publishing Trust; and the demand for it in a country whose 150,000,000 are all potential readers is enormous.

We came to a village. There was the large stone mansion set aside in a park, in which the *barin* lived until the peasants drove him out. Now, it was the village soviet house. Each wooden izba rose from the earth as easefully as a tree. A moss-like down garbed its heavy grace, heightening the unity between house and grass and loam. Beyond the aspen copse the field rose with a great herd of cattle to a hill, and the hill touched a cloud immense and white and still, and the sun tinged it from the end of the sky. We went into a forest and came at last to a cottage crudely but harmoniously cut from the bare logs.

At a round table on the porch sat several men and women and half-grown children. The men were professors. One taught mathematics, one taught philosophy at a Communist academy; the third, a pedagogue, was a dominant force in soviet education. The mathematician was a man under thirty; his experience scarce spanned the Revolution. He looked like a poet, loose-limbed, nervous-handed. I spoke with him in German. It was clear that he lived in his subject with the freedom of a poet writing a metaphysical poem. Communism troubled him not at all; he accepted it as any man accepts the traffic rule of his city. When I got to Berlin, I mentioned this man's name to a great German physicist. "He is one of the best," I was told. "He is one of the most promising men in Europe." I was learning of the pride which the Soviet Union takes in the progress of pure science.

The pedagogue was older, a man of mind. The plump indolence of his body made me think of certain characters in Chekhov or Tourgeniev. How could that soft body run with the proletarian dictatorship? The head, yes, might conceive the Rev-

151

olution; as did the intellectuals of old Russia, whom Lenin crushed at the bitter moment when they were challenged, no longer to *think,* but to *act,* the Revolution.

Very real is the dictatorship to-day in Russia; it was unreal in the presence of this ruminative man. I felt in him what I felt in almost all the intellectuals aged more than forty whom I met in Russia: wistfulness, pathos, resignation. Within that man's soul, there must have been a struggle; and when the official Communist emerged, something was dead within him. Brilliantly and faithfully he did his work. But I could hear within the didactic words of his acceptance the murmur of a plaint, could see in his eye the glimmer of a memorial candle. He talked carefully; he measured me long before he could decide how cordial he dared be, not trusting his intuitions. He was a man who never dared forget himself, lest some individualistic note from his deep self, which he had passionately labored to forget, should ring against the willed music of his official life and shatter its brittle structure. I pitied him, sensing the endless strain of his elected way.

By contrast, I thought of another Party man whom I had met just the day before, while I was roaming around the purlieus of Moscow. This man was a proletarian; he lived with his family in the cellar of a wooden slum in Drogomilovo. He showed us the wet hole in which his sick boy had to live. He was bitter in his criticism of the housing committee of the district. There was altogether too much bureaucracy, he said, in the soviets and the trade unions. A year ago this fetid house had been condemned: and here he was still. Too typical, he assured us, of the difference between his Party's programme and its deeds. This man belonged to the new world, body and soul. He was not afraid to criticise, because he knew that his connection with the ruling proletariat was organic. Perhaps the timidity that I found everywhere among intellectuals in Russia was due less to censorship than to their own inward insecurity? Perhaps, when there were literally no more "outsiders," Russia would again speak out—and again fearlessly dream?

The philosopher at our party of professors taught the history of metaphysics. He explained his course to me in pedantic French. It began with Plato; and ended with Marx, Plekhanov and Lenin. Every system was interpreted by the materialist dialectic. Only such systems were studied as helped to prepare the young Communists at his academy for the immediate work of propaganda. This professor spoke with complete assurance, never doubting that his words revealed to me the acme of intellectual perfection. He did not share the painful reserve of his friend, the pedagogue. He was a little man with fish eyes and a fish mouth which scarcely moved when he spoke. No sensibility, no insecurity, fretted his dullness. I have met such men all over Europe. In Germany, they are likely to be Lutheran preachers or petty magistrates. In France, they might be the Voltairian mayors of small towns; in royal Spain, they were priests. Whatever they are, they conform with the State faith. Thirty years ago, this Communist philosopher with equal certitude would have taught the history of metaphysics to rich girls at the Smolny—beginning also with Plato and tracking step by step the doctrine that at last emerged into the Absolute Truth of the Greek Church.

We sat round the table. There was tea and bread and salad, sugared fruits, and delicious vodka. We strolled down to the river where the philosopher was building a house which he wanted to show us. (You can build, even "own" a house in the Soviet Union, provided its value does not exceed a certain sum—I believe three thousand roubles. You join a "building co-operative," paying a fixed tithe from your wage for a span of years. The house is yours for life; you can even deed it to your children provided they pay rent on it and actually use it. At their death, however, it reverts to the Union.)

My questions about his courses had been boring the philosopher. He was like an astronomer compelled by courtesy to explain to some persistent ignoramus how he taught his classes that the earth is a planet and the sun a star. Now, as he climbed into his unfinished house his face warmed and his body grew young. "This is my study." "Here, we are going to put the sleeping-porch . . . all screened in." It seemed to me that the Communist "priest" was glowing with lust of ownership like any bourgeois.

I thought again of yesterday. With Maurice Hindus, I had made a pilgrimage to the famous Nunnery of Novodyevichi, on the banks of the Moskva. Within the ancient walls is ruin. The grass grows rank, graves are strewn among old buildings. And the religious houses, beneath their gold domes, look unkempt. Here had lived Boris Godunov; here Peter the Great had hanged three hundred rebel troops beneath the window of his recalcitrant sister. Here for four hundred years the nuns spoke the dogmatic Word of Russia, and the Word rose in ikon and stone to convince the people. The Revolution had swept away the dogmas grown too rigid and narrow to hold the life of man. Now, the convent is an anti-religious museum. The ikons are still there—among the finest in Russia. What do they reveal of the faith and the folk that made them?

The form is almost always external. The stress in color and light is upon the golden halo or the jewelled robe of the Saint. The body within the robe is flat; the features of the face, the articulation of the hands, are without plastic vigor. When a religion is humanly experienced, its pictorial art (if it permit one) reveals the incarnation of its spirit *within* the pictured bodies. Witness the faces on the *Porche* at Chartres or the torsos on Athenian temples. In the ikons, symbols also of a national religion, only the surfaces live; face and form are unquickened. And this is merely another proof (Russia is full of such proof) that the Orthodox Church, even in its hale days, was alien to the people. They did not, like the Catholic peoples, experience the Church: they merely accepted it. Had they felt it, the bodies of their ikons—not the halos and regalia—would have been plastic. And the reason for this must be that the elaborate Greek dogmas never became symbols for the living aspiration and experience of the Russians. There was contact of course; the Church somewhat expressed the spirit and flesh of the folk; never wholly.

Beside the ikons, the Soviet officials have placed cartoons displaying the priests and nuns as they sucked the lifeblood of the people or—with the Tsar's aid—trained guns upon the crowd, themselves softly barricaded behind crosses of gold. And there are placards explanatory of the ikons. As Hindus read them aloud to me, I kept my eye on the picture they were supposed to interpret.

"Here," one read, "is a picture of Heaven and Hell, the delights of the former, the tortures of the latter. Heaven was reserved by the priests for those with money to buy prayers; Hell was the portion of the poor."

A half truth, of course; a false caricature of the Christian religion. There is a new dogma in Russia: every historic scene, and every ikon, must be interpreted to fit it. From the premises of class war and of culture's economic determination, it follows that Heaven must have been reserved for the rich exploiters, and Hell for the poor exploited. The premises read more intelligently—of course—in the works of Marx, Trotzky and Bukharin. But it is the *placards* that speak to the people.

Is there not an analogy between the simplified dogma of the ikon and the simplified dogma of the placard that refutes it? The ikon also is a placard, speaking straight to the folk. It says: "You must pray before ME to be saved. You must buy and light candles before ME." This too is a caricature of a great truth—the truth at the heart of Christianity. Its essence, as it is embodied and brought before the people by the organized Church, is deformed. The deformation, subtle at first, and "necessary" for purposes of simplification, organization, propaganda, becomes immense, becomes hard, and finally destroys the very truth within it. The falsehood works its independent life upon the people. And the people, enslaved to the false form, are deprived of the truth they yearn for; and live unnurtured.

Is there not a similar hazard in the militant ideology of Soviet Russia—the rationalism which is mis-called "dialectical materialism"? What may become of the relative truths of great men like Marx and Lenin—men who were the first to disclaim dogma and to stamp their doctrines as a method of action bound to shift as the scene of action shifted? Walking beside the little professor, this day, who taught philosophy to the young Communists, thinking of the new "truths" in Novodyevichi, in the official Soviet papers, in the official speeches, I pondered this danger. In the need of bringing the light at once to the Russian people—a need made acute by Russia's state of siege within the Capitalist encirclement, and by the prevalence within the nation of the old racial habits —is there not danger that the Communist truth take an accessible form which is *half-truth?* that the half-truth harden into a lie? that a new formal falsehood stifle Russia?

To-day, the surge of the young struggle gives instinctive health to Russia. Russia is healthy, because it is wholly moved by simple nutritive and instinctive needs. There are so many tractors to be built! so many roads to be opened! so many stodgy church-laws to be burned away, in order that men and women may breathe the fresh air of their emotional natures. It does not seem to matter what Russia thinks;—it really would not matter, if Russia could go on forever in its present dawning. But when the pause comes? when the press of foreign capitalism is either broken or becomes the norm? when the farms have all been collectivized? when there is wheat and milk for every one, and the factories of free men produce in a few daily hours all the vast nation's needs? when every woman has been sexually freed, and every child in Russia is a child that is wanted? What then, if Russia finds that the battle cries of a war that is over have become its truths, and that these truths have become official dogmas to which life in its depth and its breadth gives the lie? How, then, will the young Russian look on the old ikons in the Novodyevichi? Will he perhaps not find them, in their essence, terribly familiar?

4

We went to the Author's Club for a drink. The twilight was warm, and the garden before the generous old mansion was crowded with writers, most of them under thirty. In that setting, my friend's Ford was as conspicuous as a Rolls-Royce made entirely of gold would be in the United States. In the centre of the garden was a tennis court, but although the sidelines were packed no one was watching the game. Indeed, from time to time, one of the four players held up his serve in order to listen to the literary argument of a group near him, or to take part in it.

Upstairs, Gorki was making a speech. The windows were shut, and the room was packed to the sills. The heat was almost unbearable, but no one noticed it (except me). To have opened a window would have let in the racket from the garden; Gorki's voice was weak, and these men and women were there to hear Gorki. Even their breath came silently, as the hundreds of eyes bore unswerving upon the frail, gaunt man before them.

Gorki's face is intellectually vapid, and his

blouse hangs loose about his throat and shoulders. He looks like a Russian Saint whom many years of moral discipline have so removed from intellectual problems that he need no longer choose—no longer think. Yet he is thinking. He furrows his brow, brings an emphatic fist against the table. He must think, not to find the truth, but to express it. I was struck by a frailty that seemed more of the spirit than of the mind or body, in this man who has risen from the squalor I had seen in the Millonki of Nizhni Novgorod. Gorki, whose work may have been lacking in æsthetic depth, was alway massively human: yet now, he seemed almost a feminine figure! The reader may laugh when I say that he reminded me of a bride: within the wrinkled body of this man was a spirit that had surrendered to a great force, and in surrender had found the peace of ecstasy. Gorki was blissful. Each day, he wrote his pæan for the papers; on numberless subjects but forever with the one refrain. The man of bitterness had found a happy ending for his bitter stories. And the result, as he stood there, was anodyne. The gall of his tales had been their kernel. When he created them he believed in no release from pain: he believed only in life, in bitter, unsolved life. Now, he believed in the Communist solution, the Communist answer to all questions. He was a saintly man, perhaps a great man. But what he was giving to his rapt audience was sugar water.

Moscow has only two great newspapers, *Pravda* and *Izvestia:* organs of the Communist Party and of the Politburo. There is far less variety of opinion in the public press to-day, than there was in the darkest Tsarist days. But this is not due to Communism, it is not due even to the war psychology which the Union with its encircling foes must foment: it is due principally to the want of a tradition of free speech in Russia. If there was more freedom at certain epochs of the Tsars the reason is that there was less efficiency or less need to enforce official opinion. If there is no freedom of speech to-day, the reason is that a people is not revolutionized in fifteen years, even by the profoundest of revolutions.

I explained to a young Communist one day (a bright student of Edison destined for a mechanical career) that in the New York papers every morning one might find every possible shade of judgment on all possible subjects. He shook his head, as if I had revealed an amazing flaw in American efficiency.

"I don't see the use of it," he observed. "Every problem has a right answer. It seems to me the press would be serving the people a lot better if they found out each day the right opinion on each important subject, and printed only that. What is the sense in printing a lot of different points of view, when only one *can* be right?"

Intellectual absolutism, and the acceptance of it, is engrained in the average Russian. But perhaps the want of that flabby relativism which goes by the name of liberalism in the West and which is so often nothing but a want of conviction, is not an unmixed evil.

The Russian's proneness to regimentation is a mental habit, arising from centuries of living less in a society than in a cultural herd; it is undoubtedly one cause for his emotional acceptance of the Soviet regime. I saw a pretty symbol of this trait, one evening at the Opera. During the *entr'acte,* the audience (workers, students, petty officials) went into the foyer. Quite unconsciously, *they fell into line* and began to circle round and round the large hall, in order! I know no other crowd in the world which, during a theatre intermission, does not remain individualized in little groups, standing or moving every possible way.

Because of these inherent Russian traits, the intellectuals and the intellectual arts of the U. S. S. R. are in a peculiarly dangerous position under a proletarian dictatorship which encourages (and makes effective) the habits of the masses. I was

through Russia. Perhaps before I return, I may have my answer.

The little that I saw of Russian painting did not thrill me. My friend, the critic Evgeniy Lann, insisted on taking me through the Museum of Native Art; and I saw no single work, since the days of the classic ikons, which impressed me as important.

Up to Peter's time, the painting was largely ecclesiastic, with the Byzantine influence the strongest. But the true Byzantine was seldom equalled in Russia; the native forces seemed never able to converge, with the borrowed ideology, to make a great plastic art. After Peter, France, Germany, England crowd out the Byzantine. But the Russians produced no masters. The nineteenth century seems to have imitated all the schools of Duesseldorf and Paris. Spectacular realism without æsthetic form prevailed. The Revolution released a hectic revival of all the twentieth-century radicalisms of the *rive gauche* and of Central Europe. I have never seen a sicklier display of painting. Do the Russians lack power in pure plastic? That is another question to be cautiously answered—later.

I saw nothing on the stage of Leningrad or Moscow—nothing significant—that does not hark back, *as stage art,* to Stanislavski, Kamerny, Vachtangov, Meyerhold, etc.—all men who won their greatness in Tsarist Russia, at the same sources which created Aksakov, Gogol, Ostrovski, Tolstoi, Chekhov, Dostoievski. A literary plastic—a plastic of action: here Russia has been strong. It seemed to me that the modern theatre was living on the accumulated past of the great days. Perhaps I was wrong. I was in Russia during a theatrical off-season.

Every one was saying that the Russian film has (perhaps temporarily) lapsed. The pictures I saw were indeed like imitations of the mighty works of Eisenstein and Podovkin. And the reason—as for so much that is disturbing in the Union—is *war conditions.* Not propaganda. Propaganda did not harm Eisenstein and his masterly partners. But the U. S. S. R. needs foreign money to buy machines. No stranger can imagine the passion of this need. The Union is encircled by a hostile system; only by producing the tools in which that system is strong can it protect itself from invasion, slow or swift, military or moral. And only with money can it produce the tools. Films are a means of bringing money into Russia. They must help buy tractors and engineers. Therefore, Russian films must be saleable in Europe and the United States. To this end, they must not be too "unkind" to the Western taste. They must have at least a "taint" of conventional plot, and not too stark a dose of Russian values.

But only by comparison with its own Homeric past has the Soviet film fallen on evil days. The "industry" is pure and simple, because it is an organic part of the whole proletarian movement. Perhaps nothing more pointedly contrasts Sovkino with Hollywood (for one who has been in Hollywood) than an acquaintance with a famous Russian star. A dinner at the home of a high Hollywood lady is of course a grand affair. Her home is a palace, more sumptuous by far than that of any mistress of the seventeenth-century Bourbons. The long table is set for seventy. Lords and Ladies, Wall street magnates, Senators, society matrons, popular novelists, are shrewdly shuffled among the great ones of the film. Every guest is stiff and proper, and stupid (even those who are not really stupid), until enough champagne is drunk. Then, anything may happen, anything may be discussed over the cut crystal and real lace naperies, with one exception: there will be no exchange of ideas on art or life. The actors are peacefully at home reviewing their jobs with the cotton brokers; the scenarists see eye to eye in their business with the sporting Duchess from England and the red-nosed Senator from the Southeast. . . .

Now make the leap to the home of Emma Vladi-mirovna Cessarskaya, a famous Sovkino artist. She lives, of course, in a single room. The table at which she serves us supper is beside the beds of herself and her husband; the oil stove where she has prepared it with her own hands is behind a white sheet in a corner. Her collation consists of a delicious omelette, beet and cucumber salad, black bread and jam, and Caucasian wine. Emma Vladi-mirovna wears a severe black dress, cotton stock-ings, and a single ring—an heirloom—on her ex-quisite hand. She is a girl soberly devoted to her work, who accepts life as a hard place from which one wins experience, pain, joy, even ecstasy: not "success." Yet she is ambitious, she loves to be praised. But when she shows you the "stills" of her new picture, you think of a school girl rather than of a star, so simple is her anxiety for ap-proval; and of an artist, so true is her standard of values. Behind her is a large bookcase of un-painted wood, containing translations of the classics and all the great Russians from Pushkin and Aksakov to Bunin. At the table sits a Com-munist deputy from Paris, a New York journalist, a couple of young Soviet officials, two girls and myself. The talk is both gay and deep. Here no one is afraid to speak his mind, for every one's place in the scheme of things is sure. The humble room is integral with Russia; its life is close with what is vital in Russia.

It is rank injustice, of course, to compare Hollywood with Sovkino. To Hollywood come the worst of America: the boys and girls with the shallowest, shrillest ambitions. They want coin, show, success. They are distinguished from the boys and girls they left behind in the home town not by greater humanity but by a lack of it: the girls are less womanly, less ready to lose themselves in love for some humble fellow and to give him children, the men are discards from the nation's industrial and intellectual fabric. Hollywood is peopled by "artists" emotionally cold, intellectually dull, even sexually a bit below the average at home: and Hollywood films reflect the spirit and calibre of those poor creatures who make them. In Moscow, it is the nation that makes the films: whole-bodied, whole-minded men and women who have gone into the pictures, not to escape life and win brass but because the new world is luminous and articulate in them.

What I feel, sitting in the room of Emma Vladimirovna, is what I feel everywhere in Moscow. Go to any other capital in the world: in a gathering of its intellectuals or artists, you are cut off from the core of the national life; in a gathering of politicians you feel not only remote from the country but that its spirit is being stultified and betrayed. In Russia, wherever I was—even among officials—I was at least close to Russia.

Perhaps this is a common trait after a revolution? I have felt something of the sort in Mexico. Should I have felt it also in the United States, in the first decades of the Republic? . . .

5

While I was in Moscow there took place in the Writers' Club a series of meetings at which the leaders of all groups discussed in careful papers the problems of the author's place in the Soviet Union. I had found complete candor only among pure proletarian Communists, muzhiks or outcasts with nothing to lose. Most of the writers with whom I came in contact lived insulated in a reticence I could not pierce. These meetings were historic, because every writing man was urged to speak his entire mind on the subject which has haunted the intelligentsia of Russia for fourteen years.

I knew that I would learn more with my eyes than my ears, so I was happy to find myself seated in the first row of seats on the rostrum. On my right sat a leading critic who spoke English; on my left was a poet who spoke French; directly behind me was a novelist who knew German. I did not lack interpreters; but what counted most was the unimpeded view before me of several hundred writers, standing or sitting in the narrow hall.

I recognized my two classes. Most of the older

men and women were intellectuals with an individualistic background; to a great extent the youths were "proletarian" writers. Among the former group were faces that recalled Dostoievski, Nekrasov, Gerzen, Chekhov. The Russian writer, I felt, must have been almost a class apart with feature and expression which I now read as I had read his works. Here was true individualism: mind and emotion so evolved as to touch the universal. Here were men who had pursued their thoughts till they attained true concepts, who had refined their feelings till they touched the cosmic essence within personal emotion. The world of action was separate from these men, yet not spiritually remote. Only the motives of money were remote from them, as from a company of children. And there was something childlike in the pain stamped on their luminous homely faces. It was a passive suffering; the *passio* of acceptance. Like children born in an unhappy home, they could do nothing; indeed they knew nothing beyond the constant atmosphere of trial.

Now the thought came to me that these Russian writers were of a race which had been European! Doubtless a group of authors in nineteenth-century Paris or Vienna or Madrid would have shared some of these traits. These were survivors of the *clerks* who created cultural Europe and who created the democratic values which at last destroyed that Europe! In the West, they had been wiped out by the gradual process of two hundred years. In Russia, the destructive process had been delayed, the intellectuals had still been able until 1917 to live in their essential world. Then annihilation was upon them. It was the fate of these survivors in Moscow, who now sat before me, to suffer in their own persons what the same caste in Europe had suffered slowly, during a century and a half.

The faces of the proletarian writers—mostly boys and girls in their twenties—revealed the same mild yet fertile homogeneousness of feature —like an unwritten page and a fallow field— which I saw constantly on street and farm. But unlike the intellectual writers these boys and girls had supple bodies; and on their eyes and mouths there was the mark of *will*. Will was almost absent from the faces of the intellectuals; and is not writ large in the common proletarian. The will, for instance, of a factory group is not yet stamped on the average factory person. It is conspicuous in the Communist, in the young Communist; it was conspicuous here on the countenance of the proletarian writers. In their elders, I felt substance, intellectual, spiritual—and decomposing. In the youths, I felt little substance—but a ruthless drive.

Four men, that first evening, aged forty or more, poorly clothed, with luminous sharply individual faces, read papers. They attacked the "literal" method of producing proletarian letters. Literary art was a chemical process. If one wanted a rare essence, one did not begin with it; one took all the raw materials at hand and refined and combined, until one got it. The spirit of world Revolution was an essence—*the* essence today of Russia. The more free the artist was in his employ of fact, fancy, theory, even heresy, the more sure he was to produce that spirit. If he tried to begin with it, he would end with only a substitute or a dogma. . . . Or literary art was an organic process. Like any growing life, it must be allowed first of all to live *in its own terms:* to force it outside the rhythm of its being was to kill it. If Russians had faith in their Revolution, they must believe it to be cognate with Russian life in its freest and deepest manifestations. The free growth of Russian art could only serve it. . . . If the Revolution was a spirit that lived, it must grow—and change. It must evolve from the whole experience of the people; from the untrammelled experience of the poet. Writers like Gorki and Leonov had written far better proletarian work— work far more vitally of the Revolution—when they were concerned only with their own reactions to raw Russian life, than now when they deliberately pared down everything they wrote to a Marxian conclusion.

The audience listened perfectly: at times, they smiled or interjected courteous words of assent or dissent. When each speaker was done, he was applauded mildly. A lean dark man came to the rostrum. His Jewish eyes burned, his hands shook. He was a Communist who had been a Soviet official and now taught literature in one of the universities of Moscow. He spoke extemporaneously for an hour. (Meetings, like plays and buildings, and intervals between meals, are long in Russia.) He attacked the anti-Marxian ideology of the four speakers. They talked as if individuals could create the dialectic stream of history! Writers, like every one else, must be technicians—or nothing. By means of technical intelligence, they could give adequate form to the social need of the hour, or measure and hence midwife the social trend: by making the mass more conscious of what that trend must be, they could help the mass to be delivered of its own future. *And that was all*. The historic need of the people, for instance, was that kind of food-production which required tractors: therefore the engineers modelled and put forth tractors. The historic need of the people was a certain kind of book: therefore let the writers produce it. The *factory* was the archetype of every creative act in the socialist world: for the factory represented group collaboration, conscious intelligence and methodological will. The proletarian writers must emulate the factory.

The shrill voice stopped, the fluttering hand subsided: the passionate little Communist stepped down. Without knowing it, he had given voice to a pure mystic sense of life: he had pleaded that the writers serve the Dialectic Law as his forebears served the Torah. And the assembled modern Moscow writers rose in applause.

Three of us walked slowly back to my hotel. The Strasnoy Boulevard was dimly lighted, and exuberant with people. Women packed the benches while their children slept, enjoying the warm night. The wooden booths sold kvass and beer and candy. The populace was a tide rising, surging. On the Tverskaya, the Soviet buildings lay in gray silence: the Lenin Institute was a vigilant shadow. The reformed street was like a wall defending the lyric crowds of Moscow. Walking through the crowds, we three had not spoken; now, under the silence of the darkened official buildings, we began to talk.

"Yes, the problem is complex . . ." said the poet at my right.

"The Communist had a majority with him," I observed.

"Quantitatively, yes. But do not misunderstand the applause he received. The mass of young writers *want* to agree with him. After all, if he is right, they are sure to be able to do what is expected of them. But they admire the work of the four men they listened to almost in silence."

"A world is literally being created here," I said; "it is hard to be part of the travail. Who knows which men are of the blood that is lost, of the placenta that is discarded; and which are the new creature?"

"The problem is even more complex than that," said the critic at my left. "We are not merely the new life and the living mother from whence it springs. We are the midwife also. Who knows which men are the old tissue; which the new; which the ministering hands? In this birth, if the mother dies, the child dies. In this birth, who shall say at what moment the placenta can be discarded; and what blood can be lost safely?"

"Yes," said the poet, "biology will not provide an image for our Russia. Biology is far too simple."

6

Revolutions are the friends of youth; more precisely, they are the foes of age. In industrial cities, the revolutionary centres of the Union, one sees few old people. The terrible years of military Communism wiped them out; and those who survived famine or insurrection fail before the ruthless discipline of the new order. The old that still live are hidden away in the flats where perhaps they earn a corner in a closet by cooking and cleaning for the younger roomers; or have joined relatives in some musty village not yet transformed by Revolution.

The streets, the industrial shops, the collective farms, the public places, surge with the song of youth. Youth that is allowed to be free is beautiful; and Russia's youth has found a wondrous freedom. It is given wholly to a faith and to a labor that enlist every hour, every loyalty and dream. The freedom of each young human part of Russia is the necessity of serving the whole. It is the one real freedom to which a person can aspire:

the freedom that comes of knowing and joyously enacting one's place within the human group.

The youth of Russia have accepted Communism. They alone have begun to live it as a conscious Way of life. I saw them everywhere in Moscow; and whenever I was with them, my questions slumbered, I was happy. With them, and with them only, I felt as I had felt among the proletarians in the factory or in the Leningrad streets. The Revolution is a mass movement toward the reign of intelligence in all domains—economic, sexual, æsthetic. Yet in its early stage, its energy is still instinctive. The least reflective groups and the most lyric—workers, soldiers, children—are carrying the Revolution. This is a paradox: the kind of paradox that proves the life in the U. S. S. R., and that gives hope. A movement toward Reason that had no mass emotion to propel it would be still-born. Similarly, the surge of Russia's children will die away unless its intellectual programme is adequate to the full feeling and dreaming needs of mankind.

One late afternoon, there was to be a meeting, in the great Soviet House, of the Moscow Pioneers and Communist Youth. The former correspond to our boy and girl scouts (with what a difference!) the latter—the Komsomol—are the immediate feeding body of the Party. The director

of one of the great plants had given me a ticket.
My interpreter was busy (it was his subscription
date at the Art Theatre). So I went alone.

For two hours several thousand children, rang-
ing in years from eight to seventeen, walked and
sat and discussed their vivid problems in the wide
lobby outside the auditorium to which they would
march when the Show began. I was immersed in
this green-golden sea of Russia's children. From
the white walls, portraits of Lenin and Krupskaya
looked down on us: and huge paintings of early
conferences of the Commissars in the Smolny, or
of that first Petrograd Soviet in October, where
Lenin had stood in the rostrum and said calmly:
"Now, comrades, we shall begin to build Socialism."

The children paid no attention to me. They were
too busy. I was able to sit beside a group of them
on a sofa: shift to a cluster standing in the middle
of the floor in earnest consultation. What busied
them? Only one subject: the Revolution. Each boy
and girl in the packed lobby was a soldier; more,
was a creator. They consciously believed that the
future of the world of workers—the human future—was to issue through their minds and
bodies. Is it surprising that their eyes had a lovely
light? that their faces shone with a serious resolve
which the tenderness of youth made poignant?

There was nought solemn about them. Plenty of laughter met the grim visage of Lenin, the ponderous loom of Marx upon that wall. But they laughed out of fulness, security, sweet strength. Most children laugh when they succeed in forgetting their work and their duties: these children laughed because they were aware of the splendor of what they had to do.

The girls and boys mingled without the slightest tendency toward sexual division. This too I have never seen before. There was no pairing; and there was no grouping of antagonists or hunters along sex lines. They came together according to their needs: a school soviet, a workshop committee, a collective adventure in truck farming outside the city attached to some city mill. Each need made a social unit, holding both boys and girls. And I noticed also that when some lad was being scolded by a girl comrade—perhaps a higher officer in his club—it did not occur to him to resent being worsted by a girl; nor to the other boys to defend him on "sex-chauvinistic" grounds. Yet, like an exquisite aroma, the sense of sex pervaded. Unconsciously, the girls took delight of their budding bodies, and the eyes of lads were warm on their blond tresses. Unconsciously, the hard maiden rondures glowed in the atmospheric pressure of hard male bodies. All their mind, all their will, all their emotion, was given to the single cause whose intricate parts their separate deeds embodied—the cause of Socialism. But their acts moved mellow in a glow of sex that worked like a lubricant within them.

A band struck up at each end of the huge lobby; the thousands of boys and girls fell swiftly into file. I had woven in and out among them for two hours; they had not noticed me. Now I observed a group of members of the Komsomol talking and looking at me. They reached a swift decision, just as the long line began to stir; and a youth all in black, from blouse to boots, came toward me.

"Tovarishtch, do you speak German?"

"Yes," I answered.

"I will find you a place in a box, and act as your interpreter if you desire."

I thanked him, but was not surprised. I had never yet ventured alone on the Russian streets or in a tram, without finding some one who seemed to feel my need, and who helped me.

The great body of youth, gay with banners, faced a line of grim-mouthed men on the platform, and sang the Internationale. Then, they sat in a silence marred by no murmur and no stirring. For two hours, they had argued and laughed and paced the lobby without tension or disorder. Now, in equal ease, they sat silent.

The orators were politicals, for the most part second-string men, typical, doubtless, of the new bureaucracy. They poured forth all the platitudes of the placards and the papers. Capitalism was dying; unemployment was universal save in the U. S. S. R.; by millions the workers of the world were joining the Communist ranks; in desperation, the Capitalists lynched every worker they could lay hands on, and were preparing the next World War, etc. One speaker—an old war horse who had been a Commissar in the early days and now headed the Anti-Religious League, filled his speech with malicious allusions to Trotzky. (There are country fairs to-day in Russia, where the muzhiks are invited to hit "Trotzky" in the head with a ball and get a prize—the equivalent of "a good cigar.") The speaker knew the suppressed tenderness of intellectuals and youth for the exiled hero.

"Why do certain Communists go wrong?" he shouted. "Because they do not stick to the strict rules of Marxism-Leninism: the rules that give birth to enlightenment, to Socialism, to Truth. . . ."

His talk was intellectually on the level of a Methodist exhortation. It was better only because it had vitality, not an outworn creed, behind it: because it had youth before it.

The orators spoke into the amplifier, and the amplifier was out of order. At times, it sent such a roaring and vibration through the vast hall, that the words were drowned. At times, it turned the words into a brassy din signifying nothing. I felt a symbol: in conveying truths to the public, the amplifier distorted them, made of them a huge confusion hideous to hear. The amplifier, I reflected, symbolized the politicians who were one the world over. But nowhere in the world was there such youth as this—the youth indeed of a reclaimed mankind. And this magnificent youth was listening, in utter silence, to these politicians! What did that mean? Of what was that the symbol?

One bright morning with autumn in the air, Hindus and I had wandered about the Khamovniki, a river suburb where Tolstoi lived (the gloomy box house still stands). We came to a section where concrete flats were building. The streets were torn up; and their irregular and arbitrary plan upon the dump-filled meadow reminded me of the Bronx. There were a number of drab institutional houses in the chaos—one of the universities of Moscow!

We went in to the office. It was filled with girls; there seemed to be no difference either of years or purpose between the scholars and the office workers. A student was detailed to show us through. She was a woman of eighteen, pure proletarian of course (else she had not been granted the privilege of study). Her room was narrow; a grand piano filled most of it, leaving space for a single bed and a chair and a table. The piano had once stood in some banker's or merchant's salon, and murmured Chopin in response to fastidious fingers. In the narrow bed slept both our guide and her husband.

"Aren't you crowded in that bed?" I asked.

"Oh, no. You see, with the piano, there is no room for a big one." The girl had made what is the conventional choice in Russia. What is physical comfort compared to a piano—when you want a piano?

This university was a world. We went through store rooms, kitchens, butcher-shop, bakery. We sat in a dim basement dining room made bright by the eyes of the students. We visited the *crêche* and the dormitory kindergarten, where students who were mothers kept their young. Everywhere, only students: they dressed meat, they dressed babies, they balanced books. The university was a little world at work, integral and serene in its relation with the Soviet Union. Deep down in the Ukraine, there was an enormous kolhoz—a collec-

189

tive farm—which sent produce directly to the university, and the students went down there in groups for their vacations or to teach the peasants. Even the *crêche* was a conscious member of the U. S. S. R. Lenin looked down on the bright-hued cribs, and gay posters proclaimed to the children that the *bourzhui* of eld were ogres and that their immediate present land was Kingdom Come.

The same easeful order, here, that I felt wherever the Revolution worked. These young people were the children or the grandchildren of muzhiks. And I had seen the muzhiks in their dirty villages, or squealing like stampeded pigs before a problem so simple as getting on a boat. Yet these children moved in an order that was effortless, because it inhered in the cast of their mind, in the lilt of their emotion. Again, the paradox of Russia. What inward miracle was this that led from the muzhik to the children of the muzhik? I remembered that evening at the opera where I had seen a hazard crowd spontaneously fall into line. Not order, that; but regimentation, and easily understood in a land of social chaos since the one is the mere antithesis of the other, its natural reaction. But there was no regimentation in this university. These students were free and mature. They had lovers, they had husbands, some of them had children. And while they fulfilled their studies and their personal lives, they ran their school, they directed the building of new dormitories, they carried on a co-operative exchange with a huge farm in the Ukraine. They worked in seemingly effortless order, because their acts were of the same cadence as their thoughts. The Hindus taught that magic is a change of attitude. A new cast of mind and emotion had worked the magic of these children of the muzhik.

We had swapped guides several times as we went from house to house. Now, at the end of our visit (when you visit anything in Russia, be prepared to see *all*—no detail of routine, no apparatus, no store room will be spared you), we were in the hands of a girl built round like a peasant mother. She worked in the kitchen when she was not studying medicine. Her dress was a dingy gray, not free of grease, and her blond head was moist with the steam of cookery. But her body was hard like springtime. I liked her. Since we were leaving, she felt it her duty to accompany us to the tram. As we trudged through the unpaved field, she asked questions.

"What do American girls do?"

"They work in factories and offices, when they have to."

"What do they do, when they do what they want to?"

"They enjoy themselves."

"How do they enjoy themselves?"

"They go to dances, to the movies; they eat candy, they 'pet.'"

"Don't they have any work which they enjoy?"

"I doubt it . . . as a rule."

"Why do they work?"

"To get money, of course."

"What do they do with the money?"

"They spend it on themselves."

"Don't they think of anything but themselves?"

"Not often."

"Why do they think they are alive?"

"To have a good time."

She did not understand. Her eyes said clearly, that she found these girls a dull lot; that probably for reasons of my own I was maligning them.

"How do you spend *your* spare time," I asked her, "when you are not studying medicine or working in the kitchen? Surely, then, you enjoy yourself?"

"Of course." And she explained how she spent it: she had a class of illiterate mothers, every night. Also she had her Party meetings (she was a Young Communist). And there was a lot of reading to be done, along non-professional lines.

"What sort of reading is that?"

"Marxian theory," she answered.

"Do you always enjoy yourself?"

"Oh, yes," she murmured.

Our tram was about to leave.

"My class for illiterate mothers is only an hour." she said. "Then I go to my room. Come and see me."

There were many times in Moscow when I forgot the streets; all I saw was this tide of youth rising above them.

7

I stood one early evening alone in Sverdlov Square, waiting a tram that would carry me to the famous Park of Culture. I had my instructions: to take tram "Г." But "Г" did not come. Every half minute there was a "17" or a "20" or a "Ф." The crowd poured out the front platform; an equal crowd pressed in at the rear one, while a third mass packed the car. No "Г." I was getting impatient. Close by me I saw two young men, with a girl. They too had been waiting for some time, and as I watched them they turned and looked at me.

"Park Culturyi?" I asked in what I thought was Russian. They smiled and nodded. "We're going, too. We'll take you," they said plainly.

A car, not the "Г," pounded in. One of the boys and the girl took my arms and like football players hustled me aboard. When I tried to pay my fare, they protested, and thrust my coppers back into my pocket. The girl had the dimmest smattering of German. What was most understandable was her laughter, a laughter natural as the voice of a bird, yet intelligent and shrewd. The two young men had the tense, serene and passionate clarity of Communist students.

We got out and walked. I understood them to say that this tram went near the Park although not directly up to it: tram "Γ" was too infrequent. We stood before a huge enclosure in which lights blared with music. Great rivers of men and women flowed in the gates.

I put out my hand to thank my friends, not wishing to disturb them any more. They refused to shake hands. "Zusammen," said the girl, "we're going together." And when I tried to get in line for the entrance tickets the boys pulled me away.

So we spent the evening. We strolled through the quiet throng. We watched the dancers from Kasakstan. We saw the parade of Pioneers. We munched tomatoes and drank tea. We listened to a band of soldiers as they laid down their instruments and sang revolutionary songs. We watched the amazing "Children's village," where mothers can leave their young for an hour or a day, in the care of professional teachers, while they enjoy themselves with their men. We mounted a huge wood tower, sat on a strip of carpet at the top, and came sliding, twisting, screaming, down the smooth chute. At one of the innumerable bookstalls, we exchanged presents—a portrait of Lenin, a collection of Moscow views, swearing comradeship forever.

How we managed, I do not understand, for the boys knew only Russian and the girl the slightest German; but we learned a great deal about each other in that evening's stroll. They knew the exact size of my family and the color of my wife's hair. They knew the sort of books I wrote, how much money I earned, and how many rooms there were in my New York flat. And I knew what the young men were studying, their place in the Communist ranks, their views of the Five-Year Plan, of China, of Poland. The girl, who was the sister of one of the boys, was married to an engineer in the new Socialist city near Nizhni Novgorod. She had a baby son; she came to Moscow every year for a vacation. She was not a Communist: it meant too much work, "Communists are too solemn—look at my brother!" She liked to have a good time. She was having a good time.

The evening was warm with friendship. Without effort, we were close; we were four human beings, and no conventional law, no social fear, had set up barriers between us. Love is as common as the sun; it shines as naturally in man and woman. It bound us tenderly together. Doubtless, we should never meet again. What of it? Love has no covenant, makes no demand. It is the texture of human sharing; it was the substance now of three men and a woman walking, laughing, struggling to talk together, on a Moscow night.

IV

THE BODY OF LENIN

THE BODY OF LENIN

I

The most impressive spot in Moscow is Krasnaya Ploschad, the Red Square. As you enter it from Sverdlov Square, you have at your right the immense Kremlin wall with the Kremlin churches and palaces above it: before you, more than half a mile away, at the Square's farther end is Saint Basil's Cathedral—Kram Vassilya Blazhennovo: its nine gyrant domes and its triangular spires standing against the sun like an intricately petalled giant flower. The government buildings at your left you will not notice. You will be aware chiefly of how Saint Basil's and all the buildings of the Kremlin, even its turreted walls, are dwarfed in the Square's vastness.

Krasnaya Ploschad is a perfect symbol of old Russia. It is entirely enclosed, yet conveys the sense of the infinite and open: it is formed by buildings that bespeak the stages of Russia's iron authority from Ivan to Lenin; yet its character as a whole is none of these, is not historical at all nor governmental: it is prophetic. The Square appears to be empty, except of some brooding germinal force: empty of all but the future. It is the exact antithesis of the Place de la Concorde of Paris. This, despite its size, is shut: the buildings are walls, the pavement is parquet, the sky is tamed into a ceiling. The whole is an exquisite *salon;* the home of a completed culture. The Moscow Square is all sky, all virgin earth: its buildings are dwarfed in the enormous vagueness.

Every day, if only for a few moments, I came to the Red Square, and studied Saint Basil's. It fascinated me, I felt that it held a deep Russian secret. It was erected by Ivan the Terrible in the sixteenth century to celebrate the Muscovites' conquest of Kazan from the Tatars. Ivan was so pleased with it that he rewarded the architect Barma by putting out his eyes: he did not wish the artist to be tempted to repeat himself or to diminish his perfection with a work less perfect.

The first experience, as I look at the church, is of exuberance. The onion-shaped domes, each rising from its tower to a different height, each grooved in a different rhythm, each differently jewelled, are clustered like the bulbs of flowers. But almost at once I feel that they are no mere architectural maze; they belong together, they spell a unitary form whose meaning is as tranquil as the individual syllables are flamboyant. The domes are delicately and fantastically rondured; but the towers from which they bloom are geometrically figured. The triangle, the rectangle, the semi-circle, are the predominant substance of the towers. Yet I observe that the towers are not of the church's basic structure: like the domes they are lyric thrusts from a foundation. They rise from a roof as the stalks of lilies rise from soil. The body of the church, below the roof, is low and squat as a cellar. It is pressed down and dwarfed by the immense flora, above it, of angular towers and curved domes.

Saint Basil's is conscious work of art. The problem was to admit the barbarous energies of Russia, yet master them to a strict form. The result is a portrait of a people teeming with crude potency and held by a tyrant whose hand is steadied by a religious dogma. The body of the building is stifled like a muzhik crouched beneath a heavy load. The load is the splendor of spire and dome. Unlike the Gothic, this is no aspirant structure, rising from and lifting up the nave: these are domes strange to the church body which wins no glory from them. Strange like the old nobility of Russia to the inchoate human mass on which it rested. The building is a dark pitiful thing supporting this strange splendor, which could not have risen and could not stand without it.

As I gaze now, more consciously, on Saint Basil's, it seems to move. I see the base of the church sink into the ground. I see the overweening superstructure flame into inordinate extravagance. Then, a change. The body rises, grows generous and light, although holding its prosaic form; for as it grows, it absorbs the spires and domes until the whole barbarous Byzantine bloom has disappeared.

I analyze this trick of my seeing eye and learn that it comes from the fact that the church is æsthetically *unstable*. The tensions of squat fundament and flaming tower do not balance. The body is static: it neither rises into the superstructure nor draws it down, it merely *bears* it. And the superstructure is not dynamically responsive to the base on which it stands. My mind's eye, finding this lack of true polarity insufferable, has worked on Saint Basil's—as history has worked on the world of which it is the symbol.

Now, I go into the church, and I learn how the symbol is perfected. *Saint Basil's has no interior*. Its nineteen altars are dark, low, narrow, giving no hint of the superabundant towers. The altars are a mere set of praying holes. The church, then, literally, is all surface! I read the final sentence of the symbol. The dark church body, Russia the ecclesiastic nation, has no true content. The towers of the theocratic Tsars, rising solid from the roof, have no relation with the church body. Look on their external splendor and you forget the people; enter the body of the people and you lose sight of the splendor. The towers also with their stolen energy are incomplete, inorganic: they lack the third dimension, being a mere surface and a burden on the body.

The Kremlin wall is the west flank of the square. Below it are trees and irregularly levelled earth suggestive of the fields that matrix Moscow. The wall is crenellated, and rises in periodic towers above which one sees the chaos of palace and church within the Kremlin. The palaces for the most part are Italian; the churches are Byzantine and baroque. The Kremlin is thus a discord above the pure expanse of battlemented wall. Perhaps the square gives the impression of emptiness, not merely because it is immense but also because its architectural forms annul each other. In the Kremlin shadow separated from the wall by a rise of earth, is the tomb of Lenin.

It is gray and red marble, massive, severely simple. At first it appears unrelated to Saint Basil's. But as my eyes gradually learn the message of the Krasnaya Ploschad, I find kinship between the antagonistic buildings. Both in a way are tombs; both are masses with no interior. The exuberance of the domes of the church has been withdrawn into the body of the other: where Saint Basil's flames into air to celebrate a transcendental Christ, the tomb of Lenin thrusts deep into earth to hold the body of the new earth savior.

In terms of the dialectic so dear to the Soviet Union, church and tomb are related as thesis and antithesis: but Russia's synthesis is in neither. The church is all surface, flowering with spectacular bulbs of color; the tomb is without surface, sinking into the ground like a root. All the old Russian buildings give the same impression of huge and varied surfaces, lacking in content: most of the new give the sensation of mere mass, lacking in surface. Why is this?

Russia has depth. I think of the infinite depth of the Russian sky, the infinite expanse of steppe. Lacking the limit, these are surfaceless. But organic life must have frontiers, must have a definite surface. Russia's lack of surface has symbolized its want of organic (cultural) being. I think of the native muzhik: he also is without surface, being without contact with men and worlds beyond his intimate own. He has lived a subterranean existence within his izba, within his Russian field. Drag him forth, as the Soviets have done, and he is frenzied by the world's touch like a flayed man. I think of the greatest, the most Russian writers: they too reveal depths without surface. Aksakov's portrait of the ancestral estate, Gogol's Dead Souls, Goncharov's Oblomov, Tourgeniev's Bazarov, Chekhov's Cherry Orchard, Tolstoi's inchoate land (in War and Peace) swallowing the alien *grande armée* like a vast stomach; all of Dostoievski. . . . These works are an apocalypse of life's womb. Unlike the tragic works, equally profound, of Greece or Spain or France, the souls in these Russian books lack *social context,* which means that they lack surface and are not wholly born. When the social form is given, as in the intellectual world of Chekhov, the urbane world of Tolstoi, it is alien to the inward drama; it is not the outer limit of the inward life. Only in Aksakov does the social frame integrate the life of the people. But this is a vague body—the obsolete patriarchal manor. Its heart is the grandfather—the master; and around him, wife, sisters, children, serfs, animals, trees and fields, form an inchoate orbit bound only by their subservience. Compare this rudimentary surface with the complex relationships in Sophokles, Dante, Shakspere, Racine, Balzac—in whose persons, if one touches their manners, their social and political ties, one is in immediate touch with the deep heart.

The exclusive surface then in old Russia's official arts—church building, ikon, etc.—was compensation for the want of surface, of completed breathing form, in old Russia's cultural chaos. More clearly than before, I understand new Russia's passion for the machine. The machine, binding every part of a people with every other part, fulfills its social body: gives it the surface of completion. The machine is itself a surface of man's will advancing on the objective world and transforming it part by part into man's social body.

Russia, even more than old pioneer America, needs surface: the delimiting factor that brings organic life to a human mass lost in a continent. More even than new America, it worships the machine which promises to give it surface. . . .

3

I have come to my last evening in Moscow. It is seven o'clock, my bags are packed, and there is nothing to do except get to the station by half past nine. Yes: there is one more thing to do, and the time is right for it. I put on my coat and go up to the Red Square.

When I came in to Northern Russia, the twilight lasted until nearly ten: now, in Moscow, it is getting dark at seven. A clear night lies cool above the Square, ready to submerge it. Saint Basil's colors are already pale, and the Kremlin stands white above shadows. This is the hour when Lenin's tomb is open, and when the populace may see his body.[1] The line double-file, as every evening, stretches from the tomb a half mile south to the porch of Saint Basil's. There it turns and comes most of the way back to the tomb, redoubling nearer the Kremlin wall and reaching the great Gate which is almost parallel with Saint Basil's. It is a line fully a mile and a half long. A quiet line, dwarfed in the Square. At the tomb stand two militiamen to see that no one slips in at

[1] It is preserved against decay by the injection of some embalming chemical from China.

the line head; otherwise there are no police. The line takes care of itself with that quiet confidence which any happy crowd possesses.

I take my place at the tail: two Chinese boys fall in line at the same moment, one at my side, the other behind, and he is joined by a blond Great Russian whose Finn ancestry is plain. Then comes a woman in black with a lanky son. Before us are two soldiers, unlicked cubs from some far province on their first Moscow visit. We have not begun to move. Most of those near to us are silent. There is a desultory murmur between the woman and her son; and the China boys exchange plangent syllables that sound like some instrument of percussion.

The whole Square is still. The shadows beneath the Kremlin walls grow black, the walls turn from white to gray. The palace windows—offices of Commissars, and two of them the home of Stalin —glitter with little lights. Saint Basil's flowering domes draw close together and recede. The night grows thicker than the walls which melt in darkness. Across the Square a battery of arc-lights on a roof plays on the tomb; it glows like a Burma ruby. And from the stream of light, the triple line of men and women fade away, merging like the grain in a dark wood with the Square, with the buildings, with Moscow.

We begin to move. Progress is steady now. We have come close to the tomb; we turn and proceed away from it on the second doubling. Saint Basil's is now before me: it has lost all its blossoms, it is a dim tracery in the night . . . a part of the night, faintly more intricate and plastic. We reach its porch, turn again. The last approach to the tomb is straight before us.

We stop. A rustle of questions runs through us: have they closed the tomb? A gentle questioning. There is no sign of impatience or anger. If they have closed the doors—well, we will come again! But we move, in a murmur of satisfaction. We proceed more swiftly; we are marching now at a good pace. The China boys, one at my side, one behind, keep up their tambour-like exchange of sounds. Asia and America walk side by side to do homage to a Russian. This thought makes me smile and the boy at my side instantly feels it. He turns to me and asks me, in Russian, what I am? American, I answer. He is satisfied and goes back to his words with the boy behind him.

We are at the threshold, where the two soldiers stand like caryatids. As we remove our caps, the tomb takes us. Its inner threshold gleams like a dynamo. Marble, steel, bronze insignia of the Soviet Republics, are a machine, hard and sheer as we walk down in it. We descend a deep stair; the tomb's visible head beneath the Kremlin is far above us. We turn a corner and descend again. I lose all sense of direction. I have left Moscow, left the world of space. This engine of bronze and marble is the creator of abstraction. It destroys space and time. Any miracle might happen in it.

The timelessness takes shape, it is a deep stone chamber whose heart is a case of glass holding a man's body. At each corner of the case stands an armed soldier, motionless and hard as the glass. We walk slowly, looking straight at Lenin, beholding him from his right, beholding him from in front, beholding him from his left.

He lies in a soldier's simple uniform with his hands clasped on his chest. The hands are delicate and pale and long: they bespeak precision, the exquisite capacity for pain is in them and the equal power to respond to pain with exquisite method. The head is bald, its roundness bulges forward at the brow, giving the dynamic quality of motion. All thought and feeling seem here perfectly conjoined, and the sure harmony has a single rhythm, a rhythm of the march, of indefeasible direction. I look on Lenin's face. The beard is cropped short and the mouth shows. The upper lip is long and hard, the lower pushes forward in the same indefeasible direction. The features have the Tatar glint that I have seen in Volga towns. The eyes are shut, but were they open they would still be hidden. The face gleams with an intricate emotion. There is resentment in it, cold and terrible. There is pain, tender as a child's. There is intelligence, the response to both the pain and the resentment: it quickens the face, not with fire but light. And there is a terrible hilarity, the laughter of a storm ready to burst and overwhelm the world. The varying emotions merge in a calm integer: the pain has fused in the intelligence as understanding, the resentment has fused in it as will. The face is an intellectual engine fuelled by feeling. Death dims the brightness of the face, and shrinks the body. But death has made perfect the man's impersonal beauty. In Lenin's suffering, in his will to overcome the cause of suffering, in the pure methodology of mind that his will fathered, in this body of a man cleansed of the personal, I feel the embodied spirit of the Revolution.

The Red Square has changed; all the city has changed. After the hardness of Lenin's tomb, Moscow is soft; and after the brightness of Lenin's body, it is dark. I have seen, in an apocalypse, the Revolution. These streets, through which I ride on my way to the Alexandrovski Voksal are the Revolution's unborn body; Moscow is dark and soft like an unborn body.

From the old Alexandrovski Voksal go the trains that lead to Europe. Will Russia's Revolution transfigure Russia's body? Can it, unless Revolution becomes the body of the world?

V

MEDITATION ON THE ATLANTIC

MEDITATION ON THE ATLANTIC

I

Two weeks after I left Russia, I was on the ocean bound for home. I wanted to leap straight from Minsk to New York; nor should I have cared how long the leap lasted if only I did not have to alight in Western Europe. What I needed was to be alone, to digest what I had seen and felt in Russia. But a humble tourist cannot fly straight from the U. S. S. R. to the U. S. A. If he flies at all, he must stop at Berlin; and if he is in Berlin, how can he resist revisiting Paris?

When I got to Berlin I found I was ill. I had left New York ostensibly on a vacation; and here I was, thinner, thoroughly exhausted, and with a bad cold in my larynx. That was no way to get back home. I decided to spend a week in Berlin.

An old friend, for many years the editor of a liberal paper no longer in existence, heard my whispered greetings and said dryly:

"You are not the first author who has lost his voice in Russia."

But I was to learn that Germany had lost not

merely its voice but its vision. I was here, four years ago, on my way back from Poland. In Warsaw, Vilna, Lemberg, the Galician oil fields, I had been submerged in hopeless misery. The peasants, robbed of the peaceful balance of their fields and forests, between the eastern and the western cities, were coming to the towns; and their impoverished landlords were coming also. Here they clashed with the Jews who had been brought in, centuries before, to be the middlemen of the great traffic between Russia and Europe. Now the business was barred. The Jews stifled, unable to trade and unable to devise a new way of living; unable to survive in the towns and unable to leave them. The Poles stifled with them. . . . Once, on a beach at home, I saw a number of sandlice who had fallen into a hole so deep that they could not get out. They clambered up the sides, and always the loose sand betrayed them and they fell back to the bottom. At last, in desperation they began to tear and to devour each other. This scene became the nightmare shape of my memory of Poland. What a joy it had been, after that, to step out on the platform of the Friedrichstrasse! to feel the life-will of a people chastened by defeat, who were making their world over!

But Berlin has changed. It is not as bad as Poland, having greater resources, above all a better past. Yet the confusion of the Corridor between Russia and Europe—the great economic "No-man's land" from Finland to the Balkans—is creeping westward. In four years it has made Berlin prostrate and almost hopeless. A nation which has lived by the old order dies by that order's disintegration, and dares not create another.

In the Friedrichstadt, Unter den Linden, the great residential districts—Charlottenburg, Wilmersdorf, Schoeneberg, Friedenau—I saw the Middle Class which Russia has wiped out. It still has its perfectly kept streets, its shiny trams and taxis. It still lives in apartments solid as castles on the Rhine, and a good deal more *gemuetlich*. What the people of this class possess, in cultural as in worldly riches, is an accumulation of their march through many ages—a march so steady that it made them invent Progress as the law of life. But they are no longer marching. And the accumulation of their past stagnates, decays, will become exhausted, like their spirit. I felt the erosion of despair on the once prosperous bulwarks of Berlin. War could not break this folk; but their lack of faith in their way of life is breaking them. They no longer believe in what they have done, nor in what they own; yet they hold on, having no vision of a future. They accept insane rationales of the sanctity of their traditions—under charlatans like Hitler—because this nothing is their all: no love of a new sowing has yet moved them to cast their dead fruit from them.

I went to the proletarian districts round the Alexanderplatz. I saw workers, hundreds of thousands of still stalwart men and women, being examined by clerks before they received their dole. Mechanics, housewives, musicians, prostitutes, petty merchants . . . all submerged together. There was docile acceptance in their eyes. They scarcely looked at one another, crowded in the official halls; they scarcely looked at the men and women who with mild courtesy took down their answers. What did their eyes see? For the most part nothing, beyond a possible bed to sleep in and a dinner.

"Three years of idleness means ruin for any worker," an official told me. "Take a man who headed a family, worked as foreman in a mill, read Marx, ran a union: give him three years of dole and he will never work well again, he is finished."

The streets of proletarian Berlin are cold and proper. The façades of the houses are clean, the gutters are swept daily. Men without work stand in silent groups; their eyes are angry. From time to time the red in their eyes goes to their hands; they hysterically assault some well-dressed bystander or smash shop windows. Then they recollect themselves, and scatter, to suffer alone. "We will have no Communist revolution," one writer told me, "because the German—unlike the Slav—suffers not in crowds but alone."

Near the Alexanderplatz there is a square which is a labor centre. Here, during the War and the inflation, the now waning Social Democrats built a magnificent theatre. Its interior is sombre wood, substantial and strong; its plays are equally sombre. But the workers no longer see the plays. The theatre is packed by an army of petty bureaucrats—the men and the relatives of the men who feed the workers their deadening dole. Opposite is a gloomy house of gray. In the street windows are books with lurid covers: a life of Lenin, the speeches of Stalin, Soviet novels. This is the home of the German Communist Party and of its organ, *Die Rote Fahne*. The Theatre of the Social Democrats and the Communist house grimly confront each other; there is silence and hatred between them. And the workers stand idle in the shadows of their clean-swept slums.

2

I travelled from Berlin to Paris in a snug soft second-class carriage: and it was one of the most painful journeys I have ever taken. I shared the compartment with three Americans and a knickered young man from the Balkans whose gun revealed the sport, whose portfolio advertised the artist, and whose red badge of the *légion d'honneur* pronounced the gentleman. The Americans were a single lady nervously rounding forty, and a married couple from the Middle West still hale at fifty.

As the train slid from the last Berlin station, the man pulled some books from his gladstone. He opened one, and he and his wife read in it silently together. It was the Bible. He returned it to the bag, and opened an Edgar Wallace while his spouse settled to delight with the *Saturday Evening Post*.

But the single lady felt like talking. With one breath, she revealed her happy fate: she was a globetrotter, she knew China and Tahiti, Marrakech and Singapore, and she had just been in Russia. Why, the couple had been there also: in fact, they were living in Kharkov where Mr. Sloan was an engineer assigned to the almost finished tractor works. They were returning to Omaha on a short vacation. And now the Balkan artist revealed that he was master of a fluent, peculiarly execrable English, and that he was just Dying to know the Truth about Russia.

That day, they read no more in any book. While we sped across Thuringia and the Ruhr, cutting through the darkened industrial cities—Dortmund, Bochum, Essen; while we tunnelled the hills and smoke of Belgium, while night enfolded us in Picardie, the questions and answers about Russia spun an incessant weave of words. If thoughts were visible, we should have seen when we reached Paris that our compartment was filled by a huge cobweb.

The engineer had a fund of stories on the mechanical ineptness of the Russians. He gave them with no ill-feeling, as if aware that inferiority, being organic, was not the Russians' fault. The artist greeted his report with peals of gloating laughter. The engineer's wife satisfied his curiosity about food and service. He revelled over the high prices and the low standard of cooking. The globetrotter made contributions about the Russian inability to keep appointments or to make trains arrive on time. But she had praise for the hotel in

Moscow. The engineer explained how he kept out of politics: he knew nothing about the government and he wanted to know nothing.

"They pay very well and promptly. The more you ask, the more they respect you. I know a man —a good man—who was offered a high technical post. He was eager to see Russia, so he told them he'd come for $10,000. They withdrew their offer: if that's all he is worth, they said, we don't want him."

"Some Americans," explained the wife, "criticise our engineers for helping the Russians. I think it is foolish. As if they could hurt America! Why, if our men don't take the jobs, other folks will. We might as well have them as a lot of foreigners."

"The Russians can never rival us," said the engineer, "it isn't in them. We might as well help them to their feet. The more civilized they get, of course, the closer they'll come to our way of thinking."

"Inevitably," said the artist.

"Besides," the engineer went on, "most of our men are there only while the depression lasts. Give 'em a chance to earn a decent living at home, and you'll find them making a bee-line for the States. It's a mere stop-gap."

"And they *are* nice to us," assured the lady.

"They give us anything we want . . . much more than *they* have. We have most of our money deposited in dollars in a New York bank; we take only as many roubles as we can use. And we have a car for nothing—and a nice house for a song."

"How do *they* live?" asked the artist.

"Oh, terrible. At least one family in every room. Men sleeping on the floor. In all big cities."

"In the country, they live like pigs," said the globetrotting lady.

"Of course," nodded the artist.

I was waiting—waiting for one word which would reveal that these good people had somehow felt, somehow been moved by, Russia. They were good people. Did not the engineer and his wife begin each day with Bible reading? Was not the single lady so charmed by the human race that she submitted to the rigors of travel in order to observe it? Had not the gentleman been honored by France as a patriot or an artist? Hour after hour, I waited the word that did not come. No word of the human meaning of the Russian effort to abolish poverty, fear and ignorance from earth. No word of the bravery of the backward folk, daring to set forth alone to create for the first time a world without economic and spiritual slaves. Perhaps they felt that the attempt had failed? Yet there was no word of Russia's native genius—of its music, of its writers, of its profound humanity. The engineer and his wife had actually lived there: had they had no talk with maid or man that revealed a beauty worth relating? They were citizens of a progressive country: was there nothing to report about the seven-hour day, the five-day week? What of the land that gave every pregnant woman four months' rest with pay? that assured the best medical care to every one? that eliminated the insecurity of age, illness, unemployment? On such details of fact, as on the Russian theories, the hours brought silence.

I had made the vow that I would not speak; I would give these brothers and sisters no inkling that I too had been in Russia. Now, in my forced silence I felt hate welling within me. Yes: it would be sweet to take these four in the stride of Revolution, give them a chance to squeal for an instant, and destroy them. Could one argue with them? Two of them had lived in Russia; one had crossed the globe to visit Russia; one was so concerned with Russia that he held the talk to the subject from Berlin to Paris. Yet they had seen nothing, felt nothing, heard nothing. My hate was making me uncomfortable. I knew that I could down it only with understanding.

I made myself observe the four good people. They *were* good! The engineer was a handsome fellow, upright and stern: a man you could trust. His wife's plain face showed the faithful mate and mother. In early Omaha days, doubtless she had cooked and slaved for her children. The globe-trotting lady was rather short on brain, but of good heart. Life had hurt her; the little lines about her eyes betrayed that she had flinched when pain confronted her; she was alone, and escaping for-ever, forever vainly, from herself. Even the artist was nothing worse than a self-indulgent boy whom a cheap world had encouraged with flat-tery: he had never been made to grow, never been led to question whether his facile talent justified the fat of the land in which he took his ease. They were products, these four, of three phases of bourgeois culture: the American Middle West, the upper west side of New York City, and the rue de la Paix. They were unable of their own effort to rise above their culture's level. If they could not feel life in any terms but their own, it was best to blame their culture. (And it was far more bearable to me, since this attitude saved me from the ravage of personal anger.)

I thought of the Volga muzhiks. How con-temptible they would have seemed to these four civilized persons. Their rags, their feet sweating in bast or straw, their greasy caps and shawls, the mire of their roads, the grime of their izbas. . . .

And yet I knew that only the dullest of them could have spent even a day in Paris or New York without more sensitive response to the strange world than the response of these Westerners to Russia. Why was this? Was it perhaps because the muzhik was more conscious of *his own world*—its nature and values, than the artist was of Paris, the single lady of New York, the engineer of his industrial realm? We know others only insofar as we know ourselves. The peasant, the unsophisticated toiler, have a self-knowledge humble but authentic. This, our western culture has merely covered and destroyed with a patina of lies. And that is why there is more hope in the uncultured workers of all races: more hope, not because we idealize or romanticize their sodden state, but because the finished product of modern rationalist-capitalist culture is hopeless.

3

Never has Paris seemed so beautiful to me. It is because there is added to her loveliness the pathos of distance. In the past I have been close to Paris; I have dwelt in her and loved her. Now she is like a woman whom I still love, but can no more touch. A barrier has grown between us; it holds and will hold us separate forever. But it is invisible, I can still see through it the gracious forms of my beloved.

That they are subtly softening and fading, that the erosion of time and the rot of an alien era is upon them, makes the forms of Paris even more appealing! I love this city—the one really beautiful city of the modern world, as one loves one's own youth that is disappearing. Paris, autumnal flower of Europe, we too, who are grown men today, are children of your Europe. In us, who are Americans, the bloom is gone, we are stark seeds. We have fallen in the winter ground of the world, we must rot and rise to an unstoried spring. But as we meet our destiny we may look back on Paris, which is the last fair bloom of the world in whose death we are born.

4

At last I am on the steamer. We have pushed out from Le Havre against a snapping breeze, the coast of France is a dim line and is gone.

All about me sun-green water bound by sky; the perfect frame for my experience of Russia.

My meditations, as I lie alone or walk the deck alone or sit before a cognac in the chatter of the smoking room, begin to take the form of questions. There is no hurry about answers: the Atlantic is broad and life is broader. The important thing is to clarify the questions. Indeed to ask the right question is the crux of most problems. If a man in a crisis can be sure to ask himself the right question, he need not worry about the answer.

In this unconscious pilgrimage of mine, the issues for myself are great. The spectacle of Soviet Russia has deeply moved me because it deeply concerns me. My visit among a strange people on the frontier between Europe and Asia has been a visit to myself. I have witnessed a scene in a Play that is my own—and yours too, dear reader. The fate of the Person and of Culture, the fate of all that man has heroically and so briefly builded in the few thousand years of history, are the plot of the Play. The present scene in Russia is of course not final; it is not the climax: the drama has scarce begun. But the scene in Russia is essential. And that is why every modern (unless he is asleep as most moderns are, drugged and distracted into a kind of sleep)—why every modern must be moved by Russia as a man would be if he were faced with his own future.

My questions gradually fell into five groups:

I. What is the reality to-day in Russia?

II. Whither is this reality tending?

III. Is the official philosophy of Russian Communism (dialectical materialism) adequate for the founding of the new world culture?

IV. What effect must the reality of Russia have on the world?

V. What position must the American intellectual take and hold toward the embattled Soviet Union?

I. *What is the reality to-day in Russia?*

a. What kind of dictatorship rules Russia?

The government is in the hands of a very small group drawn from the Communist Party—the one legal party of the Union. Even the majority of the commissars seem to be without great power. The Union's federal ideal—a widely shared authority wielded by numerous republics and autonomous states—is a myth at least to-day, with Russia in a condition of war. It is a moot question indeed whether a highly industrialized society will not always demand centralized control. Will railroads, electricity, distribution of goods, ever work efficiently under regional management? Whatever the answer to this question, Russia is ruled to-day, as in Tsarist times, by a highly centralized political machine.

There is of course the possibility that the ruling group, if it perpetuate itself, may become a caste with many of the vices of the old bureaucracy. At present, however, Stalin and his associates are rigorous representatives, in culture, loyalty and will, of the proletariat—that is, of the comparatively small but fast-growing group of class-conscious workers in the cities.

The nobility and bourgeoisie have been ruthlessly "liquidated." Many members of the middle class remain, but always in inferior positions save for the few who had already in 1917 aligned themselves with the radical cause. The muzhiks of course are the majority class, and are not in power. By force and persuasion they are being driven into collective and (far less numerous) state farms. Their children—the inevitable rulers of to-morrow's Russia—will no longer be muzhiks; they will naturally have acquired the viewpoint of a proletariat of farm workers.

The intellectuals have passed through many vicissitudes since 1917. They made the Revolution, and at first they ruled. The defeat of their last great leader, Trotzky, was the symbol of their fall. Stalin gradually crowded out all the leading intellectual comrades of Lenin (but Trotzky is still strong, in secret, among the better class of Communist youth and even in the army). The bad days for the intellectuals, immediately following Trotzky's exile, are also past. Teachers and engineers are now included in the First Category, which makes them the economic equals of the factory workers.

b. Are the ruling values of the U. S. S. R. proletarian?

The populace accepts itself emotionally and in spirit. This simple fact points to a deep revolution; in all other countries of the West the peoples, consciously or unconsciously, do not accept themselves but aspire to the status and standards of the upper classes. But the *intellectual* values of Russia are still, to a degree, bourgeois.[1] The men who

[1]So are the artistic values. Tchaikowsky and Rimsky-Korsakov, for instance, are favorite composers of the hour: and the popular concept of "utilitarian art" is strangely similar to what we used to hear from our Victorian aunts and uncles.

made the Revolution accepted certain intellectual attitudes that rose with the nineteenth-century middle classes: their geneticism, rationalized materialism, hegelianism, etc., are now stratified in the Marxian dialectic. "Our doctrine," said Marx, "is not a dogma but a guide to action." But a people with a thousand years of dogma for its background, and in an immediate crisis, belies this statement. Marx's way of thinking, which was inevitably of his epoch, has become crystallized as an intellectual "lag." I feel, however, that this will be overcome by the vitality of a proletariat in action; above all, by a future people possessing security and leisure.

c. Is there Communism to-day in Russia?

No. The Union is in the transition period forecast by Marx. This phase is aggravated and prolonged in Russia by the need of first creating what Capitalism has created elsewhere—the industrial milieu from which alone Socialism can spring. So long as there are classes, there must be proletarian dictatorship; so long as there is an incompletely industrialized nation, there must be rigid State control:—and these are conditions contrary to Communism. Moreover, values are still expressed in Russia in terms of personal, even monetary reward. The Udarniki (shock-brigaders) and the inventors earn more *cash*. "From every one according to his capacity, to every one according to his needs"—the Communist golden rule—has not been realized. The economic and political regime is a State Socialism. But the Union's educational and cultural values (not its *forms*) are sincerely Communistic.

d. Who is happy to-day in Russia?

Before answering, we must bear in mind that the Revolution is still too young to have changed the Russian people deeply. The young are moved to-day by an enthusiasm that may not last: the old are caught in a despair that will not survive them. The adult mass whose formative years go back of 1917, are still conservative, easily led, servile in their ancestral habit of being ruled. The muzhik is still barbarous and potentially creative, by reason of the lack of cultural crystallization in his past. This crystallization is being applied at present to the young—with a vengeance. It must hence be clear that neither the joy nor the misery visible to-day in Russia can be taken as a permanent trait. With these reservations, I can make the following general answer. . . .

The class-conscious workers are happy. The office holders are happy, when their background is proletarian. The youth in town, farm and school, are happy. I detected signs of crisis in the youth (and this made *me* happy): a certain unrest due probably to the fear that their personality is suffering. This is why there is much drunkenness among the young men; and explains a certain febrile over-compensation in their performance of Communist tasks.

The old muzhiks rotting in their villages are unhappy. The individualistic artists and thinkers are unhappy (those in Russia no more than those who have fled to Paris). The surviving bourgeois are unhappy.

e. Is the Communist ideal natural and organic in Russia?

Yes, to an amazing degree. (Of course, the ideal will change, even as Russian human nature will change, with years of adaptation of the one to the other.) We have seen that the Russian people is, by feeling, *monistic:* it senses life as an interrelated whole—not like the North American as a dualistic or pluralistic order. Russia's monism, unlike the Hindu, has no transcendental trend. More like that of China, it is *naturalistic.* Yet it is suffused with mystic feeling. When intellectualized by contact with the West, this feeling comes close to the pantheism of Spinoza. Therefore Russia's passionate acceptance of Marx is not mysterious;

for Marx may be said to have turned monism from its Hegelian detour back into the direction of Spinoza.

Both Spinoza and Marx are more naturally close to the Russian genius than the dualistic Neo-Platonism on which the Russian Church was founded. Transcendental religion, dualistic mysticism, have always been dissenting movements—or a superficially accepted creed—in Russia. The peasant is pantheistic and pagan. Tolstoi's natural, ethical religion is more typically Russian, I believe, than the antinomian mysticism of Dostoievski. Dostoievski was a city man, a bourgeois profoundly influenced, despite his slavophilism, by Europe. Tolstoi, despite his internationalism and his intellectual debt to Stendhal, Schopenhauer and Rousseau, was the archetypical muzhik—the true Russian genius. In his work are implications of naturalistic monism which, when linked to Marx instead of Rousseau, and to Spinoza instead of the Gospels, again reveal the native adaptation of Communism to the Russians.

The Russians, moreover, are a people of crowds and groups; they rejoice and suffer, instinctively, together (unlike the Germans). Every village in the Tsarist days had its commune. No other proletariat went so swiftly from serfdom to Communism as the factory workers of nineteenth-century Petersburg. Psychologically also, Communism is well adapted to its first official home.

And economically, Russia calls for a collectivist society. Its fields are vast, its horizons are remote: only a people organized *as a whole* can dominate the physical vagueness of Russia. It is the lack of such dominance that left Russia impotent for a thousand years.

f. Is the Bolshevik Revolution a national movement?

Yes: and profoundly Russian despite its internationalist creed.[1] The defeat of Trotzky marked the complete and conscious *nationalization* of the Russian Revolution. And I am convinced that the Revolution in all countries must be national as well. No theory for the future can efface the cultural *facts* that the names France, Germany, England, U. S. A., America Hispana, represent. What is needed is an international creed sufficiently profound and catholic to be adaptable by the varying psychologies and economies of the world. That is why the American Communist who too docilely accepts the Russian ideology, taking its particular form of a universal need as the universal form, is not serving his cause as well as he might if, with

[1]This, of course, does not mean that it is *nationalistic*. Its vision is international and not remotely nationalistic; its form and accent is national. The Russians, indeed, have never been nationalistic.

240

less dogmatism, he were more quickened to the cultural needs at home. For it is the *home values* everywhere that must be transfigured into the energy of Revolution. This is what took place in Russia.

g. Is there kinship between the Russian Revolution and earlier movements?

Yes. But an adequate analogy would lead to innumerable pages. Think, however, briefly of Islam. The Arabs were a people spread formlessly through a desert. They had a local culture, a great literature; but they were materially backward as compared with other peoples of their time, and impotent as a world force. Mohammed came to them with a native restatement of the intellectual values and emotional needs of the day. For religion, he learned of the Jews, Manichees and Christians; for politics he went to Constantinople. He galvanized his people with a rationale for their energies and with a dynamic direction. The Arabs leaped swiftly to the vanguard of culture, and conquered a vast world. The analogies between Araby and Russia, Mohammed and Lenin, Islam and Communism[1] are plain—and must not be carried too far. The world is different, which means that its factors and values are different. It is interest-

[1] A Communist writes: "Socialism is the one god, and Lenin is its prophet."

ing to note that whereas Mohammed, despite the religious vocabulary of his day, was really a materialistic pragmatist, Marx and Lenin, despite the materialistic vocabulary of their day, were profoundly religious men. I suspect that the roots of Marxian dialectic, with its assumption of the universe as a *rational* organism (Hegel, Spinoza, the Hebrew Prophets), are more essentially mystic than the roots of Islam.

One great chief difference between the two movements is that of method. Mohammed, in the way of his age, offered a rigorous dogma to which life must conform. When life ceased to conform, life ceased to nourish the dogma, and Islam decayed. Marx and Engels, to avoid this danger, disclaimed dogma and insisted on an evolving doctrine of action whose cultural values are not posited *a priori,* but grow with the action. The Marxists who are as dogmatic as Mohammed misquote and betray *their* prophet.

h. What is happening to the individual to-day? What may happen to him to-morrow?

Theoretically, the individual in Russia can scarcely be said to exist. The ideal of collective-social progress is so dominant that it might be called the sole value. The value of immediate individual experience is discounted: and of course, at least theoretically, this deprives social value of its fundamental integer—personal value. This fallacy is a heritage (like almost all the present ideology of Russia) from nineteenth-century bourgeois Europe: a heritage aggravated by the "war-condition" of Russia. But actually, this anti-individualism is not a danger; for it is a theory that does not work. Persons thrive better to-day in the true collectivism of Russia than they do in the false individualism of the United States.[1]

Aside from theory, what are the facts about individuals in Russia?

The Russian woman, in town and collective farm, is being freed of her immemorial slavery to *Kinder, Küche, Kirche*. She has time for herself. This means that she will have time to suffer, to make tragic mistakes, and to mature. Accepting her absolute equality (not identity) with man in sexual and social life, she can afford to be a woman. Her womanliness can only be enhanced by liberation from the drudgeries of the housewife: drudgery, so far as I know, never helped the womanliness or the humanity of any wife. More womanly women I have never seen than the young Russians of the towns.

[1]These problems of the Person are discussed in *The Rediscovery of America* and in the second part of *America Hispana,* where it is shown how the false individualism of the United States leads to a neglect of personal value and, hence, to a false notion of social progress.

The family is not disappearing in the Soviet Union; it is being spiritualized, it is becoming less a matter of a private kitchen where a woman endlessly presides over a private set of pots and pans, and more the human relationship between a man, his wife and their children. Even if the child lives in a *crêche* and the parents work in factories, the family need not die; particularly as the workers' hours of leisure are increased. Family may become less an economic and sexual compulsion, more a flower of the conscious will and of active love: more intimate and more essential.

As the muzhik disappears, an extraordinary human type should take his place: a man as close to the soil and seasons as the peasant, yet with all the city dweller's complex social (hence intellectual) contacts.

The present Marxist mood, were it to harden into an effective creed, with its exclusive stress on *social* progress and its neglect of the *personal* value, would indubitably prevent the flowering of true *persons:* for the complete individual is one who knows his integral participation not merely in the social group (with its time dimension) but in the Cosmos experienced by intimate and immediate conduits—the emotions and intuitions. This "knowing" cannot be merely intellectual; it must be the fruit of the person's self-discovery and self-experience. And for this reason, Russia's present intellectual dogma is likely to be less destructive than its present experience is constructive, of real persons. Let me make this clear.

The impulse for true self-discovery arises from the need of overcoming the impediments to its solitary course which the immature ego encounters in the world. In an individualistic society, such as that of the Western nations, these impediments take the form chiefly of conflicts with other antagonistic and equally "solitary" egos. In a collectivist society, the impediments might conceivably develop not so much through friction with other egos, as through the resistance to any personal endeavor of the ruthlessly driving collective whole. The problem would be transposed, not basally changed. The "solitary soul"—the immature person—would still have to face the fact of his frustrations in a hostile environment of others like him, and would still have to learn that his problem can be solved only by a self-search sufficiently deep to reveal within himself the principle of harmony not merely with the group but with all life. Therefore, I see no cause for fearing that a collectivist society would impede the growth of real individuals. When leisure comes to Russia, individualism will be in crisis, for only the enriched individual can enjoy leisure. A new philosophy, as useful to personal growth as Marxism is useful to the proletarian struggle, should evolve.

Indeed, when I consider the æsthetic and spiritual genius of the Russian people, I am tempted to predict that their socialist society, if it be permitted healthily to evolve, will within a generation give birth to a new individualistic movement—probably in literature, philosophy and psychology. And this movement will be toward a *true* individualism, in which the social basis and texture of the real person will be understood. In the past, owing largely to the class conflicts by which society was rended, the attempt of individualism to reach the universal has resulted in the stress of the *cosmic,* and not of the *social,* basis of the person.

II. Whither is the reality of Russia tending?

a. Is true Communism coming in the U. S. S. R.?

Like everybody else, I do not know. What Russia has to-day—economic collectivism or a centralized State Socialism—will not automatically flower in true classless Communism (a *culture* based on autonomous and regional co-operation of all the people). Man with conscious discipline and mind must midwife the birth. State Socialism, in Russia as elsewhere, might abort into a political oligarchy that sustained its slaves at a high economic level, keeping the intellectual control and the power. In this case, of course, the revolutionary cycle would have to re-commence, not on the motivation of widespread hunger (which I feel is bound to disappear from the world), but of intellectual and spiritual enslavement.

The hope against such miscarriage rests chiefly on the universal education of the Russian peoples. It is as hard to conceive of the young Russians, as it is easy to conceive of the old Russians, tolerating an oligarchy. The danger signals of the present time are the absolute centralization of power, the tendency toward piece-work payment, the economic privileges of the shock-brigaders and the settling down of office-holders who already are called in certain places the "Soviet bourgeoisie." The argument that these evils are transitional can be answered only by time.

b. Can the U. S. S. R. achieve its goal alone, and surrounded by a capitalistic world?

If the goal were State Socialism, I should say Yes. With its limitless resources, the Union—provided it wards off Japan and the Western Powers for the next few years—could survive for generations despite a hostile world; particularly if China and India come within its orbit. But the goal is Communism; the passage from State Socialism to Communism is a problem in *culture;* therefore my answer is No. The political defeat of the Union must take place at once or never; for soon the U. S. S. R. will be invincible. The cultural defeat of the Union might well take place slowly, after many years of isolation.

c. What are the effects of protracted encirclement by capitalist countries likely to be?

The Soviet Union's transitional "war state" might be perpetuated. The Union might go on being ruled by a few strong men whose extraordinary power was "justified" by the crisis. It might go on exerting censorship and enforcing uniformity in political and intellectual life, on the same pretext of war conditions. It might go on rewarding men by capitalistic standards on the pretext of having to fight the capitalistic system. The Union would then become more and more isolated intellectually and more and more remote from the Communist ideal. Its critics at home would not dare speak out, lest they give comfort to the enemy; and its sympathizers abroad, moved by the dominant need of defending the Union, would not dare speak critically, for the same reason. The fixed emergency in Russia would tend to fixate the few revolutionary thinkers in the capitalistic countries into a mood of defense, so that freely revolutionary thought would not develop. Conversely, the full play of intellect would be impossible in the Union under the obsessive psychology of siege.

If this state of siege persisted indefinitely, the U. S. S. R. might become a kind of Asiatic *ghetto* on the edge of Europe. The Jewish ghetto in the late middle ages was superior in some ways to the peoples that surrounded it. But its intellectual and creative forces suffered dry-rot because of the constant need of the ghetto to give most of its energies to self-defense, and because its isolation barred or deformed fertile contacts. (The ghetto did, of course, have contact with other ghettos and this saved it.) Gradually, however, it became corrupted by the superstitions of its Gentile neighbors. It was so absorbed in combating the official Christian dogmas, that it was helpless against the more insidious infiltrations of the folk. At the close of the eighteenth century (when fortunately for the Jews and for the world it disappeared), the ghetto had acquired most of the cultural and economic evils of the Gentiles; it was intellectually stagnant and far inferior in fresh cultural activity to reawakening Europe. Something broadly analogous might occur in a Russia prolongedly cut off from Europe. Its intellectual forces would grow ankylosed; its dogmatism would harden; it would develop an "inferiority complex" disastrous to its supple evolution.

But no such ghetto is thinkable in the modern world with its universal system of exchange. Communism, I feel, will either evolve in China and then, in some adequate form, throughout the world, bringing Russia into the universal fold; or another system will issue from the present chaos and finally absorb Russia.

d. What would happen if Russia lost the spirit of Communism, and hardened into an industrialized collectivist order, regimented by a new ruling caste?

It would become a menace: an engine of irresistible might (mechanized and well fuelled) which its rulers could direct in conquest against Orient and Europe. *But this supposition disregards the human nature of the Russian peoples.* It disregards the truth that Russia has had a Communist Revolution because Communism bespeaks its native genius. It assumes that the spirit of Russia could be totally lost, while the economic body which that spirit has called forth remained.

More probable is the supposition that if the true spirit of Communism fails or dies in Russia, the inchoate peoples of the Union will once more disintegrate. These peoples were loosely held together under Tsar and Church, because of a religious-emotional bond and because they were helpless against the police of the central order. They are now achieving a high form of integration, because the promise of Communism expresses their emotional genius more deeply than their past religion. If Communism fails of its promise (with Tsar and Church buried—and irrevocably, in view of the peoples' education), the nationalities of the Soviet Union would probably fall apart. The "menace" of a potently organized Russia is therefore a delusion. If the Union is strong, it will be a menace only to Capitalism; if it betrays its own life-spirit, it will destroy only itself.

e. If Russia wins its first battle—if it abolishes poverty, establishes security, comfort, leisure for everybody—what then?

The test of Communism comes only after this initial economic goal is reached. It will come in the answer of a physically satisfied people to the question: *What shall we do with our lives?* A people physically at ease, in which no fresh creative values have instilled new cultural rivalries and aims, would lapse into disease. All the old vices of idleness (sensuality, power-lust, exhibitionism, etc.) would soon rot such a people. This is why the strengthening of the creative energy and of the creative imagination is urgent, even while the economic fight is being waged. And Russia knows this . . . knew it, indeed, even during the darkest years of civil war. On the upbuilding *now* of cogent values to replace the incentives of physical survival which still reign in Russia, depends the ability of the people to emerge from the economic stage of proletarian dictatorship into the cultural stage of Communism.

III. Is the official philosophy of Russian Communism (dialectical materialism) adequate for the founding of the new world culture?

This is an ambitious question, and its adequate answer would require a book. Yet an answer is so important to every American intellectual to-day, that I cannot avoid at least the beginning of one, despite the danger of a brevity that may seem too essential or schematic. I must, of course, assume that the reader knows the general meaning of the Marxist terms. If he does not, he should go to some source book on Marxian philosophy before he reads these few pages. . . .

The materialist dialectic by which Marx gave a progressive order to the great divisions of human events—the Asiatic, the classic ancient, the feudal, the bourgeois, the socialistic "cultures"—really constitutes a *physiology of history*. Physiology of the human body, by experience, discovers man to be an organism; and gives order, within strictly limited phases, to the being and behavior of his body. It makes no attempt to define the quality of the human organism as a whole, nor to exhaust the field of human nature. By analogy, Marx in his "physiology" of history had to assume that mankind in its historic extension is an organic body. This is an intuitive assumption (similar to what one finds in the premise of all creative thought, scientific or æsthetic), which Marx shared with Hegel even as Hegel shared it with Spinoza. But Marx justifies his assumption by proving that it works: his "physiology" of economic production and distribution establishes an order—however crude and imperfect—from the anarchy of man's historical behavior: an order which appeals to our experience and reason.

This demonstration places Marx among the great natural philosophers, makes him the peer of Darwin who brought a similar order into the chaos of the biology of species. But with this mighty contribution, Marx was not content. He was a prophet in the Hebraic sense, which means that he was a man of action. He was not content with knowledge, which he deemed inadequate even as knowledge unless it was applied. He wanted not to interpret history, but to make it.

Having proved the logical necessity (in accordance with man's organic process through the ages) of a social revolution which would abolish poverty and classes, he wanted to *move* men to that revolution. But men were not moved by intellectual theorem; they were moved by their emotions, by their *visions*. In order to carry them to revolution, Marx must therefore leave the circumscribed field of economic history; he must invade the domains of philosophy and religion which determined what men believed, what men felt and saw, and how men acted. Thus it came about, that the theory of materialistic dialectic was transformed into the philosophy of dialectical materialism: that a method of explaining human history (particular phases of the behavior of a particular animal through a few centuries) was turned into a method of explaining all existence!

In order to understand this transformation, we must not lose sight of Marx the man of action in his immediate epoch. The period 1840–1880 presented two paramount foes to social revolution: the revealed religions and German metaphysics. Religion was the defender of the reigning bourgeois Capitalist system. With its *apriori* God outside of nature, it seemed to put the burden for the institutions of the world on Deity; it moved men to suffer their present bondage by stressing the hope of happier times in Heaven. And German metaphysics, whatever its brand, always managed to concur with religion: it was, indeed, a more sophisticated Protestantism and the militant apologist of the bourgeois system. Both Kant and Hegel came to an elaborate theodicy that proved the rightness of life as it was, the reality of the *apriori* God, and even (in the last phase of Hegel) the sanctity of Prussian monarchs! Schopenhauer rejected Christianity, of course; but only to preach resignation to the powers-that-be, for Buddhistic reasons.

It was hence natural that Marx the revolutionist should find his arch-foe in the Absolute—call it God or Spirit or Idea—which seemed either to justify the social and political present or to place the burden of its recreation *outside* man's immediate endeavor. All these reigning systems of thought were, at bottom, idealistic religions. And for that reason, Marx hated the words idealism and religion: and began by calling his own system materialistic.

Sidney Hook[1] has made clear that this "antitheological" spirit moved Marx even in his choice

[1] See his "The Philosophy of Dialectical Materialism." *Journal of Philosophy*, Vol. XXV, Nos. 5 and 6.

of terms. "Every proposition," he writes, "in this philosophy is so phrased as to rule out the notion of an 'efficient' God. God is dangerous to the social revolution only if he is an active God—only if he creates worlds. And for the Marxist there is no other than 'a creating God.'" Marx attacks theology, and its subtle daughter, philosophical idealism, because they are the enemies of social revolution; he selects his terms, in order to make militantly clear their severance from the religious and philosophic words which are used to lull men to inaction. But the essential motive of this anti-theological animus of Marx must not be disregarded. *Marx attacks the church, because he wants to win for his own cause the impulses that make men go to church. Marx attacks theology, because he wants to enlist for social revolution the energy that theology controls—the energy of religion.*

Marx hates the theologians for the same reason that the Prophets hated the priests: because he is their rival for the hearts of men. Like the ancient Prophets, he wants justice to be done on earth, he wants to bring consolation to the hungry and down-trodden; he wants, above all, to make men see that they are active integers in the great Whole; and that to attain health, which is wholeness, they must enact their part, not by "vain oblations," but by deeds. Marx is the foe of church

256

and church philosophies, *because he is their rival in religion.*

We might amplify the religious impulse in Marx by developing the analogy between Marxian justice as an inherent quality of growing life and the Prophetic justice; the analogy between Marxian dialectic applied to history and that sense of organic connection between all phenomena that underlies all true religion: above all, by revealing the ethical quality which Marx mystically instilled in nature, by visioning nature as an order emerging toward justice. But we dare not linger. . . . The point we must make is that the anti-theological form and wording of Marxism found an immediate object in the world, and became crystallized. Men were priest-ridden; religion to the proletariat meant submission to economic masters; God meant a magic which, in a later life, would right the miseries of this one. It was inevitable, therefore, that the embattled Marxians should stress the simplistic meanings of their materialism: that they should, in phrase, become anti-religious and atheistic, despite the profoundly mystical and religious implications of their dialectic.

This aspect of Marxian materialism was of course still more compelling in the work among the Russian and Asiatic hordes. And it is valid there to-day. Any suggestion of "God" or

"Spirit" or even of "metaphysics" among such peoples would at once re-open the door to the priest and shut out the Communist organizer. If Marx had reason to give names to his philosophy that would serve primarily as a defense against priests, how great was the same motive in Lenin and the other Communists working in priest-ridden lands of the East! They can afford, even less than Marx, to enter into arguments about the meaning of God or of "first causes" or of "Substance." The energy of revolt must be confined to a narrow channel. The problem is one of dynamics.

We come, therefore, to certain clear conclusions:

1. The terminology of Marxian philosophy was largely formed as an aggressive defense against terms which the theologians and metaphysicians of Marx's day had made weapons of apology for the Capitalistic order.

2. The Communist stress on atheism and anti-religion in Russia is largely the result of what "God" and "religion" mean to the Russian and Asiatic masses.

3. The prestige of Russian Communism throughout the world, due to its political triumph, has tended to harden into a dogma accepted by all Communists, an aspect of Marxist thought which

is not integral to Marxism but which is largely the result of local conditions as they once existed in Western Europe or of local psychology and conditions as they still exist in Russia.

In the West, to-day, the case is other; and the effect of this hardened Marxian ideology must be different. The North American working classes, for instance, are not priest-ridden. Their superstition is not the old theological magic; but rather the new cult of the machine and the delusion of Democratic freedom. Having, moreover, lost contact with the soil, they lack that primitive sense of the Whole—the sense of the organic unity of man with life—which muzhik and proletarian retain in Russia. Thus, it follows that whereas the masses of Russia and China win from their simplistic version of Marxian philosophy chiefly a liberating impulse from priest and magic, *while they retain that primitive sense of integration with men and with the world which is the essence of religion,* the North American masses are likely to win from the same doctrine chiefly a corroboration of the shallow materialism and anti-religious mechanolatry which they have already inherited from their bosses; and in their want of essential contact with soil and self, a corroboration of the contempt for philosophy and æsthetics which is already widespread among our bourgeois, be they merchants, writers or professors.[1] In a word, the materialistic terms which in Germany and Russia were primarily designed to combat the values of the upper classes serve now to strengthen the current superstitions of the American upper classes and the upper-class hold on the American masses.

Thus it is seen, that even for its immediate functioning there is danger in identifying a great movement with a creed whose validity rests chiefly on the ground that it *immediately* helps the movement to function. The creed does not always work; and where it fails its failure strikes back at the heart of the movement. Even for its immediate needs, Communism must outgrow the terminology which arose from its first battles in Germany and their continuance in Russia . . . must achieve a statement based on a vision of life as deep and broad and flexible as growing life itself. No less than such a vision can be simplified for any kind of people, without dangerous distortion.

But there is another aspect, no less urgent, of this question of the official Communist dogma. The philosophy of dialectical materialism, as it is interpreted to-day by its adherents, must be re-

[1]The North American's lack of vital relationship with both soil and self, and its dire effects, are discussed in Part II of *America Hispana*.

vised for the sufficient reason that it is a false philosophy of life. Even if it have validity to-day in certain places as a "fighting doctrine" against bourgeois ideals, this revision—if the philosophy be ultimately false—is an immediate necessity. For the assumption that the future need not trouble us to-day is fatal. There can be no to-morrow that is not lodged in to-day: a society that neglects its adult values while it is immature will never mature, since it is the vitality of these values at present which alone can mature it. A world movement which sets out with an inadequate world-vision is certain to miscarry.

Marx, who was one of the greatest and most beautiful of men, was too busy with economic research, too distracted by his magnificent encounters with theological foes, to perfect his logic. Otherwise, he surely would have seen that what he meant by *dialectic* contradicts the implications of *materialism;* and he would have found some less ambiguous and less misleading word to replace it.

Materialism means nothing, unless it means that spirit and mind are the products of physical matter and physical process. And this means nothing unless the properties of mind and spirit are made contingent on the properties of physical matter. Materialism of this true kind had its disciples in Greece and in eighteenth-century France; and Marx contemptuously rejected it. It had been reborn in the sensationalistic materialism of Feuerbach, whom also Marx rejected. The "matter" of Marx is not a "first cause" (Marx denies first causes); it is an organic essence; and it evolves by an organic process which Marx calls dialectic. But dialectic is a process of thought. And the "matter" of Marx behaves indeed like spirit. It progresses of its own nature, it evolves justice and beauty, it creates thought that is capable of transforming its creator and of transforming matter. Such "matter," holding latently at the beginning the essence of justice, consciousness, creative thought and will, and evolving dialectically from its own nature, is not by any logic matter. Such "matter," which, since it dialectically grows, is alive, organic, is not by any logic matter. Such "matter," whose organic growth is in the direction of justice, is not by any logic matter. Such "matter" is really the same as Spinoza's "Substance"; and it would have been more reasonable, like Spinoza, to call it God than to call it "matter."

Dialectic and *materialism* contradict each other. But it is everywhere plain, that what Marx truly believed in was the *dialectic*—the life-process toward consciousness and truth. He used the word *materialism,* as we have seen, because his enemies had monopolized the words idealism and God. He used the word *dialectic* because he meant it.

The philosophy of Marx assumes, moreover, that mind and will can shape events: that they are, indeed, of the essence of events. "Up to now," he said, "philosophers have merely interpreted the world: what they must do is to change it." His, therefore, is not merely not a true materialism: it is a thoroughgoing rationalism. And every implication of the Marxist creed to-day in Russia, where conscious intelligence has been lifted to control, is that of a deliberate rationalism: *i.e.*, of a faith that the world's material form can be and must be made over by the conscious mind.

Now, if the trouble lay merely in Marx's having placed an unprecedented meaning on the word "materialism," we might accept his definition and insist that whenever he says "materialism" we shall read "naturalism" or the like. But unfortunately, Marx did not merely and consistently choose the wrong word for his magnificent philosophy. He failed to make clear that his matter *is* organic—*is* the life-entity, like Spinoza's Substance, whence both matter and thought proceed. He himself often wrote of matter in the classic restricted sense. And he thereby encouraged his disciples, the world over, to fall back on the classic meaning of matter as mechanical and lifeless; with the result that dialectical materialism almost immediately became the kind of "mechanistic materialism" which Marx himself abhorred.

Unlike Hegel and Spinoza to whom Marx owed so much, neither Marx nor his followers have been good logicians. Hegel, at the outset, gave universal properties to his Spirit in order that he might organically evolve his universe from it. Spinoza, at the outset, identified God and thought with essential Substance, so that he might evolve consciousness and divinity from his naturalistic order. The Marxists treat of a universe which is organic, progressive, ultimately conscious and just; yet, despite their unavowedly mystical and rationalistic apparatus (the dialectic), they limit the substance of that universe to a narrow empirical field (a field which even mathematical science has transcended), from which are excluded those very forces which render possible the organic, progressive and conscious traits of the Marxian world!

Is this a mere quarrel of logicians and philosophers? Would that it were! The practical results of the Marxian bad logic and of the consequently faulty Marxian metaphysic, are visible in the writings of orthodox Communists throughout the nations. The Communist revolution aspires to create a new world. That world must contain the *real* —all the real. But what if its Communist dogma admits to be real only that shallow surface which the cant word materialism allows? Such a gap between the real universe in which men live, and the part admitted by the conscious mind enslaved to a dogma, would make an ever widening gap between men's experience and the values by which they consciously lived. This gap would lead to a new dualism and would result in a decay like that which doomed the dogma, hence the culture, of Islam.

Let me conclude this too brief inquiry into a crucial problem. . . .

Orthodox Communist philosophy reveals to-day a certain dangerous fixation inherited by nineteenth-century conditions and by immediate Russian conditions . . . a fixation aggravated by the natural dogmatism of the Russian mind. But as the Revolution evolves, its philosophy must evolve. As the writers and artists and thinkers of the world, from South America to China, grow more and more convinced of the urgent need of social revolution—and of the justified political leadership of the Communist Internationale—its philosophy will evolve.

IV. What effect must the crusade of Russia have on the world?

a. What of China? India?

The orders of Chinese civilization have also broken down. An immense mass of peasants rises in chaos, the machine and the pressure of Japan begin vaguely to bring them together, and their new stirring generates a dim light within them. Out of this confusion, the mind of China (its intellectual youth) looks toward Russia. Here at hand is an order of salvation! No army of Japan, no concert of Powers, can weaken the appeal—moral, intellectual, economic—of Russia in China. Only the Soviet Union's self-betrayal within its own boundaries could betray it in China.

When India has struck free of the dying body of imperial Britain to which it is still shackled, it will come into its own intrinsic problems. The chief of these is *transcendentalism*—true core of the caste system and of India's social disease. Hindu transcendentalism is the result of man's inability to cope with a too exuberant tropical nature.[1] The introduction of the machine, which can master the tropics, must weaken this old way of escape among the Hindus. With the weakening of transcendentalism and religious dualism will come the dissolution of castes, the rise of social dissatis-

[1]See p. 193 of *America Hispana*.

faction. A new India will have outgrown Gandhi, will be ready for a naturalistic monistic philosophy and for a unitary social order: *i.e.*, for some native adaptation of Communism. Meantime, thanks chiefly to Gandhi, the Indian national struggle is being worked out in such high terms of human value, that when India enters the stage of social struggle it is bound to make a great cultural contribution to the world.

We may expect much from lands like India, China, South America, Mexico, whose still intact spiritual values will help to transfigure the World Revolution.

b. What is the challenge of Communism to the West?

To understand this question, we must first dissociate the essence of Communism from what it shares with other programmes. . . . The essential challenge of Communism is *not* the mere abolition of poverty. All forms of Socialism, even Fascism, even the planned economies of Capitalism, agree that poverty, unemployment, old-age insecurity, etc., must cease. Mere "good business" demands this, since colonial markets for the dumping of overproduced goods are bound to dwindle, and the time must come when the machine owners of each country, if they would prosper, will have to sell to prosperous peoples. Moreover, it has not yet been proven that the specific claims of liberal "planned economy" are necessarily false: or that Communism *alone* can abolish poverty. As a matter of fact it is being abolished in Russia to-day by a working system that is far closer to State Socialism than to Communism (although it must be added that the impulse making the people work is the Communist ideal).

The machine, it seems to me, inevitably leads— under whatever system—to the disappearance of physical want and to greater physical leisure for the masses. It is the character of the machine to produce vast quantities of goods and foods; to universalize the demand for these, and to require their wide distribution if the machine is to go on working. And if the world to-day, although full of machines, is full of hunger also (and of forced idleness instead of leisure), the reason is that the machine is still so young that it has not yet reshaped economics and politics to accord with its essential nature.

Before the industrial revolution, the world was ruled by minorities of men, to whom the problem of overproduction was unknown: they produced what they could, aware that the more they had the more they would profit in selling. These men, under Capitalism, owned and developed the machine.

While they went on, by the old rules, producing what they could, and the masses went on, by the old rules, blindly selling their hands for a bare subsistence, the machine began flooding the world with merchandise. The problem of sufficient production was solved; but Capitalism had no answer to the new problem of distribution and consumption. The leaders under Capitalism went on, and still go on, as if the entire economic problem had not shifted. The machine, which demands an economy of distribution and consumption, must therefore transform the Capitalistic order under which it developed.

So far the liberals agree. But the machine, ultimately assuring foods and goods to all the peoples (under whatever system), also assures their *organization* and *education*. This fact brings us to the essence of Communism as contrasted with half-way Socialisms. In all earlier ages, the masses by the individualistic conditions of their toil were kept separate and dark. The machine-run factory, the factory town, the printing press, and now the machine-run large-scale farm, bring the masses, by the collectivistic conditions of their toil, together: force them to organize, to read, to grow self-conscious. With this inevitable evolution, the proletariat will not long be satisfied with enough to eat —nor with leisure—nor even with luxury. It will want to *rule*. It will scorn all planned economies of a dominant class. The peoples of the world will insist that the world be literally theirs: that their spirit, their mind and art, shall make the world over.

This cultural programme is the essence of Communism: it reveals why all planned economies of Liberalism, Fascism, Socialism, in their stress on the problem of bread, are superficial and unrealistic. The challenge of Communism is not bread for all or even cake; not freedom from insecurity and war—all of which might conceivably be assured to the fatted underlings of some other system. Communism proposes nothing less than the recreation of the world in the unitary image of the toiling masses. With the perfection of the machine and the abolition of profits, the toil of the masses will diminish. They will have leisure. And they will employ that leisure to *create*. Communism proposes that the actual workers shall be the new world's creators and its rulers.

This is a cultural movement more fundamental than any which the world has known since Christianity began. All it needs is an adequate philosophy (and art)—the labor of the creative men of to-day—to make it a religious movement: to make it the religious movement for which the world is passionately crying.

V. What position must the American intellectual take and hold toward the embattled Soviet Union?

Surely my answer is implicit in all that I have said.

Many forces are making the world over, in science and art. Many forces, in science and art and thought, are giving man for the first time the effective means to be free. In the past, a few could be "free" only by exploitation of the many. And since none is separate from all, this meant that even the "free" were enslaved; and the cultures and religions of these "free" ones showed their enslavement. Now the many can be free through the intelligent exploitation of the new slave—the machine. The world is in travail of a new culture that will be the first *human* culture (as contradistinguished from slave cultures)—the first *world* culture.

Such a birth cannot be simple, and many kinds of men and all the nations are needed to fulfill it. Its process will be as various as the earth, as intricate as the ways of human genius. But no phase in this birth is more important than the economic, whose means is the Social Revolution. And in this paramount phase of the world travail, the leader by right of achievement is Soviet Russia.

What is taking place to-day in Russia is the

most precious social event, the most precious social life, of our crucial epoch.

Every man and woman who is unwilling that human life should be a mere bog of personal lusts, who lays claim to belief in those values which men have lived for in all ages, under such names as God and truth and beauty, owes loyalty to Russia. Russia is our time's most conspicuous stronghold in the country of the human spirit. We must defend the Soviet Union with our spirit; if need be, we must defend it with our bodies.

But this does not mean that we must intellectually submit to Russia or imitate its ways and dogmas. That would be to betray the spirit which makes Russia worthy. The American intellectual above all must beware of a false emulation, which in accepting the letter destroys the spirit. We must be loyal to the social aims of Russia; loyal to the soldiers in the revolutionary ranks, and ready to take their side in every feasible way. But above all, we must be loyal—like the men of Russia—to our own needs and intuitions. We must forge our part of the world future in the form of our own genius.